White Holes and the Visualization of the Body

Žarko Paić

White Holes and the Visualization of the Body

palgrave
macmillan

Žarko Paić
Department of Fashion Design
University of Zagreb
Zagreb, Croatia

ISBN 978-3-030-14466-1   ISBN 978-3-030-14467-8   (eBook)
https://doi.org/10.1007/978-3-030-14467-8

This Palgrave Macmillan imprint is published by the registered company Springer Nature Switzerland AG.
The registered company address is: Gewerbestrasse 11, 6330 Cham, Switzerland

Preface

If we remove the tone of the vatic dimension of speech and the tone of the apocalyptic in speech about what is to come in the arriving, it would seem that contemporary art immersed in the dark shadows of the present would lose any kind of sense of its own sovereign right to the destruction of everything in existence, including itself. Haven't watershed thinkers and artists of the modern period demanded that it should be overcome and superseded in the immanent transcendence of the world, from Nietzsche to Artaud, from Duchamp to Debord? Perhaps the time has finally arrived for us to free ourselves of the temptation of cutting art down to a profane commentary on philosophical and scientific interpretations of the world and to its being used to further social change and awareness of general change in the actual world. All these are superficial and external definitions of that with which contemporary art confronts us, still retaining the primordial understanding of creating something new-in-the-world. It is necessary to get rid of what follows when the paradigm shift from metaphysics to cybernetics is coming.

I owe my thanks to close friends and colleagues, who encouraged me to create this book devoted to mutual relationships between contemporary art, the body, visualization and the technosphere. I would like to express gratitude to Dean Komel, University of Ljubljana, Dražen Katunarić, writer and publisher, editor of the Litteris Editions from Zagreb, and particularly to Tonči Valentić, University of Zagreb, who

carefully reviewed the manuscript and provided useful language sugges-
tions with the intention of clear articulation of key assumptions. However,
the book would not have come to the light of day without the participa-
tion of my MA students. During summer semester 2008/2009 they
attended a series of lectures on aesthetics in which I discussed the issue of
the body in the bio-cybernetical framework, with special impacts on phenomenology and psychoanalysis. Finally, I would not want to exclude
Lauriane Piette, my executive editor at Palgrave Macmillan, because with
her promptness and care this book came into the public space of interaction with readers.

Zagreb, Croatia   Žarko Paić

Contents

1

Introduction

1.1 Corporeal Turn

Why have *emptiness, communication, visualization* and *body* been permanent topics of interest ever since the end of the 1980s? Are these words only metaphorical concepts for postmodern theoreticians when they want to argue about the works derived from various cultural theories? Obviously, emptiness and communication, visualization and body are closely related. But they are neither binary oppositions nor in the dialectical sense of the synthesis of contradictions. Their connection stems from the structural fourfold of the media age. Fourfold here simply designates the cluster of postmetaphysical terms/words. The identity of the contemporary world is determined by the place (topology) of difference. We should be able to say that the same in the differences hence makes the concept of identity an empty concept (*flatus vocis*). So the term might be empty when a real object is missing. If it is possible to enumerate anything covering a word such as culture, then it might take the fluid markings of a group's or individual's lifestyles.

One of the most important novels of the twentieth century, Musil's *The Man without Qualities*, already in the title describes what is at stake

© The Author(s) 2019
Ž. Paić, *White Holes and the Visualization of the Body*,
https://doi.org/10.1007/978-3-030-14467-8_1

here (Musil 1995–1996). The term *emptiness* signifies that the subject in the new relationship has squeezed the substance. That matter of things, therefore, means that the concept of a man now no longer has its substance. He is "without qualities" as soon as his spiritual substance is taken away. It focuses on how in a postmodern age the man should be considered and thought of: he is simply the mental-bodily subject of social relations and the cultural order of meaning. From this perspective, the identity is just that amazing search for the lost ground under the feet. Although the subject denotes etymologically what is sub-taken, and the substance that is sub-divided, the subject without substance seems like a body without a "spiritual eye". No doubt it is visually fascinating, but at the same time its new identity might be nakedness with no other "core".

When we ask what makes the identity of a contemporary nation, the answer will always be the same and performed by listing its attributes: language, religion, art, customs, myth, memory. So the essence of the human in the world lies in the process of being disassociated from all of this and is dependent on its political subjectivity. Without this, he was deprived of his right to be present in the world. The power of political construction (the subject) decides on the deconstruction of national features at the time of the global order of nation-states. In the global order, identities are social and cultural constructions. They are not historically immutable, but change guarantees their survival. With respect to these facts, identity should be constructed in the process of developing its differences. The same or dialectical enframing evolves to a higher degree of equivalence in differences, or shows in all of that which Heidegger calls "stability in change".

Precisely, we can say that the same (identical), which is the very concept of identity referring to the impossibility of further sharing, might be represented by a figure of the prism. Through it, light passes through different angles. The observer no longer sees the whole of the light, but only the reflection in objects. No doubt, reflections like fractals of light constitute a whole picture that opens to the observer. But it is not someone who constitutes a picture; rather, they might be constituted by it. The image of a man in Greece, the Middle Ages and in our digital age could be the same as that of a man as a being who creates images related to a subject. Obviously, regarding the way in which such an observation

works, there are only two strongly conditional "analogous" views—
"subject" and "object". It will be clear from this point that the image and
the cognitive turn are respectively taking the place of the contemporary
image of the world. The phenomena are not shown directly, and the
observer could not be in the position of a mere observer. Therefore, the
subject is completely changed by the act of perception. We know from
the representatives of quantum theory that observing at the same time
changes the observer, and from theoreticians known as epistemological
constructivists in their current investigations concerning the role of tech-
noscience and cognitive patterns in shaping the mental scapes of the
Third Culture.

The emptiness makes the underlying ontological structure of the Being
in the time of the "eternal present" (Paić 2007a). In any case, the implosion of information in the digital age creates the necessity of interactive
communication between beings. They have a role of active participants in
the network of events. Communication becomes, in addition, informati-
cally and technically produced. The condition of communicative capabil-
ity should be the visualization of information. A picture that is generated
by a technical or digital means designates an artificial image immersed in
virtual reality. It does not appear in "living bodies" as living images at the
beginning of the process of developing new media (film). The body of life
might be constructed in mediascapes. It could be named the virtual body
of life itself as the emptiness of visual communication that precedes all
other forms of human social and cultural relations (Paić 2008). The fourfold of emptiness, communication, visualization and the body corresponds, by analogy to the fragmentary identity of the contemporary age
of the image of the world, to an empty place of the imaginary, symbolic
and Real in the construction of the world of the media age. The scheme
includes the imaginary, symbolic and Real because it has a direction to
Lacan's notion of the structural relationship between the unconscious
and the language that articulates the world as the horizon of meaning
(Lacan 1996). Imagination is always representing merely the pure empty
fantasy. So the symbolic might be the empty meeting point of the signifier, the sign and the signified all the way. From that viewpoint, reality
does not mean a distorted image in the mirror as in a *camera obscura*, as
Marx has conceptually visualized the notion of ideology (Mitchell 1987:

168–172), but the virtually generated space–time events of anything that exists. The matrix of the image precedes any possible imagination, because the generated circuit of infinitely multiplied information is performed by a "new" technological reality.

As in the age of global equilibrium of all cultural differences, the question of identity in a certain way becomes a question of overcoming the boundaries in the logical, historical and real world of events, so undoubtedly the locution of what we call the *world* at the same time refers to the complex recombination of concepts–metaphors from physics, information theory and information technology. Additionally, it relates to something self-explanatory that simultaneously gets contoured, which is the most difficult to contemplate regarding the status of the world's worldliness. It goes beyond all limits of the logical-historical order of meaning. One cannot even ask about it in a traditionally metaphysical way. Nothing can be expressed about its uncanny nature, there is nothing to learn from that *what*, because metaphysics on all its historical occasions performed that something determined as accidental, mere second substance (e.g. *res extensa*, as philosophically articulated by Descartes) or an extension of nature, shape, matter. No doubt, it was always defined as something accomplished, never autonomous and never having a relationship with a higher order of meaning in which soul (*psyché*) and spiritual are operative.

This shows what emptiness, communication and visuality *are* in the contemporary age—the *body as an image or medium*. We do not assume that the body is not here a set of physiological properties and organs. It is neither an automatic nor a mechanical circuit, as it has been considered by modern rationalist metaphysics from Descartes to Malebranche, and it has been based too on a notion of nature and especially of animals. Subjectivity, in the philosophical sense, denotes the act of self-expression of the mind as a constructive power to exclude all other determinants. So the body does not think, though the brain has the role of the central organ of thought in the body. Hence it seems obvious that the body always signified only the surface, the externality, the object, the mediation between the spirit and the soul, the visible field of manifestation of the so-called inner forces and processes. Instead, nowadays we are witnessing, at full scale, the ecstasy of emotionality. With the help of cognitive psychology, contemporary emotional intelligence should be considered more important than intellectual development as a logical-abstract network of learning the symbolic structure of the world. It can all be justified in the rebellion of a disdained body and its historically "lower" functions in understanding the world at large (Damasio 2005).

Indeed, it will not be uncommon to argue that the word/concept *body* in the 1980s has been completely depleted from the speech of the basic words/notions of metaphysical history, as it were the spirit and the soul (Assmann 2008: 93). If the spirit (*logos*, mind, *Geist*) lies in the centre of philosophy to its end in allocution in the positive sciences, and the word soul (*psyché*, soul, *Seele*) descends into the inner, dark and unrecognizable field that was the beginning of the age of psychology and psychoanalysis, then the body gained its ecstasy beyond the meaning of the new order of the social and cultural practices of the repressive desublimation of the 1960s. The body is, after all, exceptionally articulated as a series of discursive practices. In that sense, the word as the basis of the text signified the beginning of a "metanarrative" about the body in Western culture as the outcome of modernity. We can talk about several different discursive practices. The new concept of culture as an identity by using them is immersed in the world itself. It should be emphasized that the term "world" has always been linguistically articulated in the medium of society and culture. The world is revealed in the horizon of meaning through language. In this way, the world marks openness as far as the possibility of a singular change of assemblage of matter (environment, beings, things) is concerned. Having a world does not mean, however, to be a disposition to some outside space–time of the world as its mere function or service to someone outside the world. To be open in the world means to have its "nature" that is not predetermined by externality, which is autonomous per se.

The "world" of contemporary art from the moment of the appearance of the historical avant-garde in the first half of the twentieth century is reduced to the social revolution of life. We must not forget that this turn does not diminish to create a new world, but only to the problem of the social revolution of the world of life. The difference between the world and what belongs to the fragments of society is therefore almost ontological. However, art wants to create a "new society" rather than a "new world". Until today in the works/events of contemporary art, society appears with the object and the reference field of its activity. Even today, many contemporary artists unproblematically use the early avant-garde procedures to bring something subversive to an artistic event such as the performance of a living body, replacing classical notions of aesthetics such as beauty and the sublime. To prove this assumption, it will be sufficient to refer to the usability of the key syntagm of the neo-Marxist theoretician and contemporary artist Guy Debord, *the society of the spectacle*. As we know, it encompasses a society of commodity fetishism of capitalist production, with the disappearance of the usable value of goods in favour of their exchange or symbolic value. The sign of identity in the society of the spectacle constitutes the media, which means the visual communication between objects as a mutual exchange enables the assemblage of things. Who is the subject of the society of the spectacle? The answer is no one else and nothing else than the body as the spectacular posture of what is left of the human (Debord 1994; Best and Kellner 2001). The remainder remains indivisible. That is the reason why now all the remaining possibilities of a media-constructed world are taking place in the body itself. It can be understood why the space–time of the society of the spectacle has represented the virtualization of reality and stability in the change of what we call the moment. Everything is happening at the moment, starting with how time could be shaped by global capitalism. A matter of fact shows the largest possible impact on the distribution of time and space in the world of life. In between the space–time of this distribution, the body enters the horizon of all translocations in the cognitive capitalism of today's network. So the body was already pre-medially constructed as follows:

1. The medial relationship between what is the substance (Greek *soma*) and the sign (Greek *sema*). In the digital code of new media, the body is decoded in virtual space–time as a somatic-semiotic field of writing, meaning from a new social and cultural environment. The notion of environment is not only related to the natural environment but primarily to the surrounding world (*Umwelt*). Such a world is systematically determined by the institutional networking of subjects/ actors of communication. Everything related to the body is inevitably becoming a communication product (sexuality, fashion, art, sport,

spectacle). Body culture in the media environment is at the same time a new body of techno-culture. The semiotic of techno-culture becomes a binding theoretical interpretation of the body as a medium. The sign, the signifier and the signified of the body give the "meaning" in the context, or, better said, in the new signage environment. Only in the physical communication of different socio-cultural groups does it have its place and symbolic value. Outside it could be only reduced to somatic extensions: meat, matter, surface, an externality.

2. The construction of gender/sex in a fundamental "ontological" turn testifies to us that the body might not be essentially defined, but rather should only be confirmed as a body of a man, woman, transsexual/gender subject by its social and cultural actions. Today we can assume only that the basis of every feminist and post-feminist understanding of the body as "inscription" becomes the notion of transformation of the body, which starts from the epistemological process of social constructivism; so nature is not a matter of self, but what we call the "nature" or "substance" of the body constructs the subject (Butler 1990, 1993; Grosz 1994). Simone de Beauvoir claims that being a woman is not the way in which one is born, but rather something one becomes. The subject in social constructivism is more mature and is always socially and culturally determined (subjectivity of women, subculture, minorities). Body performance, therefore, creates the fundamental medium of its openness to the world (Paić 2007b).

3. There has been a relocation of the meaning and deconstruction of the power order (political, social, cultural) in recognition of the body as an oppressed subject of history. This is the basis of today's postcolonial theory (Bhabha 1994). So it is not only a feature of the universal rebellion versus racism and the ethnocentrism of Western globalization, but it is a sign of the construction of new hybrid identities. The body is no longer "white" (the hegemony of Western civilization as a universal path of progress/modern development), but it is not even "black" in the meaning of the political-cultural struggle for the freedom of recognition of another identity. If the body means a cartography of new hybrid identities, then its fluidity and total openness extend beyond the limits of the semiotics of the body. The signs of such a body are no longer related to the essentials, the universal, based

on the Father/Law of the adventure of history. Almost everything becomes twisted, deployed, decentered. We can determine the relocation of bodies appropriately as a constant struggle for a new acknowledgement of "black" in the "white" world. And at the same time, the "white" world becomes a reflection of the new transnational, transcultural and transgender identity. The purity of origin and the primordial "nature" of the body were destroyed in various fragments.

4. New technology now has absolute "authority", which has been explicitly shown during the reign of the new media as new information and communication technology functioning in the decentralized world network and reaching out to quite other dimensions. The body as a network or the complex order of structures and functions constitutes culture in the global age as post-culture, or as a virtual horizon in which what is left of world history is happening now. We should name that matter a body which operates like a "machine". Its socio-cultural organization represents a transition from the time of the *transgressive body* (Arthur Kroker) to a pure object, or in the form of the cyborg as a link between biocybernetics and real life (Featherstone and Burrows 1995). In this mode of appearing, the body is de-saturated and de-subjective to the limit. So it becomes an artificial life or a technologically alive body that thinks, feels, embodies. Deleuze and Guattari's term "desiring machines" disappears from the horizon of the world in which the world is mechanically constructed as the language of things. The language becomes, therefore, a new reality of a digitized economy of desire. Here we must not neglect the influence of Wittgenstein's late thinking and his concept of language games (*know-how*). Without it, anything would be deficient in view of the question of language and image in the age of the technosphere.

The term *corporeal turn* which I am using here should be comprehended in analogy with the notion of a visual, cultural and pictorial turn in philosophy and theories of contemporary art from the perspective of a new notion of the image (and visuality in general). The turn towards the body encompasses a whole set of discursive procedures and it cannot just be reduced to an epistemological turning point in social sciences and humanities. Quite the contrary, the discovery of body dynamics in contemporary art and politics, among other things, marks the path of liberation from the long-standing metaphysical tradition in which the body is incorporated in the condition of obedience, subjugation and objectness. In this way, it shows that what Deleuze calls "the plan of immanence" enters into all areas of life and changes our way of knowing the world. The body cannot be understood as a sign of something else, but only as an autopoietic relationship between the system and the environment. Being in the world means being connected to other creatures, starting from the proximity of interconnected bodies as visualized events of freedom (Paić 2011).

1.2   The Uncanny Event

The uncanny event of what we call contemporary culture is a separation of love from desire, the substance from a subject, surface from depth, black from white. So the paradoxical effect of this separation was that instead of merging and uniting love and desire, substance and subject, surface and depth, black and white, it all comes down to a visual fascination with the body without the remainder of the sublime. The ultimate result of this long-lasting process of turning the world into a naked body is determined by the *emptiness* of all meanings, understanding and comprehension. Baudrillard's interpretation of David Cronenberg's film derived from J.B. Ballard's novel *Crash*, which comes with the technological orgasm of death itself in car crashes and the delight of fascination with bodies without organs, in addition to the pure aesthetics of objects, appears to be pessimistic when it might be precisely all of that which corresponds to the assemblage of contemporary culture:

> From the classical (and even the cybernetic) viewpoint, technology is an extension of the body. It is the evolved functional capacity of a human organism which allows it both to rival Nature and to triumphantly remould it in its own image. From Marx to McLuhan, one sees the same instrumentalist vision of machines and of language: relays, extensions, media-mediators of a Nature destined ideally to become the organic body. (…) in

its baroque and apocalyptic treatment in *Crash*, technology is the deadly deconstruction of the body—no longer a functional medium, but an extension of death: dismemberment and mutilation, not in the pejorative vision of a lost unity of subject (which is still the perspective of psycho-analysis) but in the explosive vision of a body given over to "symbolic wounds," a body commixed with technology's capacity for violation and violence and in the brutal surgery that it continually performs in creating incisions, excisions, scar tissue, gaping body holes (…)—a body with nei-ther organs nor organ pleasures, entirely dominated by gash marks, exci-sions, and technical scars—all under the gleaming sign of a sexuality that is without referentiality and without limits. (Baudrillard 1991)

The body is fragmented because the fragile whole is also fragmented. It seems that Baudrillard's fault had to be properly corrected. Marx did not understand technique merely as anthropologically neutral. However, it is not just a means or extension of nature in capital. Technique signifies a means of work, and technology has attempted to realize the means/pur-pose of production for production in a rational mastery of nature. So technology represents the media or scientific means of cultural dissemi-nation over the world at large. Insofar as the "new McLuhan", as they called Baudrillard, makes a mistake when reading Marx in *Economic and Philosophic Manuscripts of 1844* from an anthropological perspective, it is forgetting that in *Capital* we are faced with overcoming the social-humanistic role of technology (Sutlić 1987). This is not the only thing in Marx's view of "human nature" in relation to the realized potentials of industrial capitalism. Something else would be much more significant. Namely, we have already seen how the ranking of signifiers changes, how high technology, unlike mechanical engineering, becomes more and more autonomous in the power of changing social relations. Man is no longer the "subject" of this change, as he is not at the same time the "object" of that performance.

The problem opened by the transformation of technique–technology into the medium is not merely the problem of constituting the body as a machine on the horizon of metaphysics, as Baudrillard adds in his lucid analyses. It seems that those are far more inspirational than all recent theories of representation in visual culture, from the horizons of psycho-analysis to interpretation of the paradoxical disappearance of the body in its two modes of appearance in contemporary art: (1) contingent and (2) existential. The first means "being" the body as the organic substance of the body, and the second means "having" the body as a spiritual-existential circle of openness in the world (Paić 2006: 259–265). How do we at all come to argue that the paradoxical disappearance of a body is going on in advance? The question of the "ontological" origin of the contemporary world as a digital world of the technical image stems from the premise that the body-in-the-world should only be possible when the world becomes a technical-technological body without organs. The great commitment to the body in Western culture up to the modern era is a reliable indicator of this assumption. Philosopher Wolfgang Welsch in his analysis of the transition of aesthetics to the design of the world of life points to the paradoxical way of presenting the body today (Welsch 1996: 319–320). In the telematic environment of the presence of the body at a distance, one can only ask the question of whether the physicality of the world has materiality at all. The body rises in the centre of the world only when it becomes the decentered subject of desire. In other words, the body is not always perpetual and forever given. Hence, it is neither a substance between substances nor a bodily organ. We have to conceptualize the body as a contingent-existent event of overcoming the oppositions of metaphysical categories from the very moment of the construction of everything that is in the subject–object opacity.

Therefore, Baudrillard's example of interpretation of Ballard's *Crash* shows us something that seems more radical than the transformation of the media as a means of mediating information or extending nature for a purpose, or the complete circle of meaningless exchange of messages. When, instead of love, desire itself has attempted to be absolutized or disappears in the fascination of oblivion, when instead of being erotic pornography is universally embodied in the body itself, it becomes the uncanny logic of winning the object over the subject. In the aforesaid essay, Baudrillard argues that there is no further need for psychology anymore because emotions are reversed by visual impacts. But there is no desire or libido anymore either. The body as a lust engine assumes what is left of its desire in its substitute organs. However, we detect the pure enjoyment of fascination in the image of the Other. On the screen, they penetrate the holes, but not the real persons. "Live" in real-time and virtual space, sex is practised in all imaginable forms of experiment which previously separated sadism from masochism, the perversion of the transgression of the body itself. We should be able to note that the consequence could be the radical disappearance not only of bodies as images in the traditional sense of rendering and presentation, but rather something that is now paradoxically elevated to the rank of the only true interpretation of visuality as unconscious and the body as a sublime desiring machine. Baudrillard in the analysis of the novel and film *Crash* came to what he needed and should have come to; namely, the end of the interpretation of the very odds of psychoanalysis in general explaining the contemporary world as the order of "simulacra and simulation":

> Here, all the erotic vocabulary is technical: not ass, prick, or cunt, but anus, rectum, penis, vulva. No slang, no intimacy in the sexual violence, only functional language: equivalency of chrome and mucous membranes. And it is the same with the congruity of death and sex: rather than being described with pleasure, they are melded together into a kind of highly technical construct. No sexual pleasure, just discharge, plain and simple. And the copulations and semen which fill this book have no more sensual value than the outlines of wounds have the value of violence, even metaphorical. They are only signatures. (…) Sexual pleasure (perverse or not) has always been mediated by a technical apparatus, by a mechanical process, of real objects but most often of fantasies; it always involves an intermediary manipulation of scenes or gadgets. Here, sexual pleasure is the only climax; in other words, it operates on the same wave-length as the violence of a technical apparatus; the two are homogenized by technology and encapsulated into one object: the automobile. (Baudrillard, ibid.)

If there is no suppressed lust, then what is the initiator of sexual intercourse between people which has become an aesthetic zone of empathy? Sexuality as the last zone of so-called shock and provocation of contemporary art in exchange for prohibited zones of social norms and moral rules becomes the visual communication of a body-object with other body-objects. If we take it seriously, then we should argue that all bodies are being reduced to a clear sign without the real signifier. Further, if therefore there is no feeling, desire, libido, there is no reason why psychoanalysis should any longer explain the visual language of the contemporary world. The media are not "unconsciously articulated as a language" (Lacan). They are "what" precedes any possible communicative realities at all. This "what" is no longer a transcendental thing-in-itself or "sublime object of ideology" (Žižek). It becomes the *fact*, directed towards suppressed or accumulated desire. That "what" happens as though it still "has" something from the remainder of the ubiquitous in the totality of everything that is. Sexuality and obscenity as the original forms of communication in the emptiness of the visibility of the body are reduced to the fascination of the image. However, the problem is *as though there is still "there"*. But what? With whom we are really fascinated, if not with the remnants of the supernatural in the image of aesthetic bodies capable of being broken apart? Are we fascinated with the act of "emptying" into holes or the event of total disappearance of the body in the apocalyptic event of all physical death? Let us make that "finishing" an orgasmic act of dying in the white true end of the body's history. The meaning of this ultimate, ending up as pure, is that nothing bothers to throw its light at the start of this fascinating event. In the new cosmological theories about the emergence and future of the universe, the idea of gnostic dark matter (*nigredo*) is constantly being renewed. Dark matter is at the same time the negative white, the absolute light that disappears into the time wormhole with galaxies. In the painting of the neo-avant-garde artist Anselm Kiefer, *nigredo* becomes the sublime point of the beginning and end of all art (Pedraza 1986). We can argue that the ultimate point of visualization of new media simultaneously emerges in bringing the whole world to pure information.

1.3   Objects and Things

Media are not the means/purpose of human existence, but rather an ephemeral event of the construction of the world as a universal technical image. Who, however, governs the subjects and objects of the event? Who or what holds this new mystic power—image, word or number? Is there anything concrete about the embodied power of capital, or is it "what" is beyond the abstract of the technology-visualization technology? Does painting depict an object of the subject, in the sense in which

Baudrillard says that the uncanny rebellion of contemporary art is that objects are deconstructing us nowadays?

If so, should an alternative to the current trend of returning the subject to philosophy and cultural theories be a return to the object? Neo-Lacanian psychoanalysis and the increasing interpretative influence of Deleuze with the body enframed as a machine, precisely desiring machines and the "body without organs", have led to the almost binding nature of the interpretation of visual arts and visual communication in contemporary research on new media which starts from the assumption, developed by Friedrich Kittler, that the language of the new media is just a new technical language of the universal and the unconscious (Mersch 2006: 185–206). Is the body at all possibly comprehensible from such a psychoanalytic "ground" in language? In contemporary visual communication, that language does not speak anything more important to its speakers. It can even be said that nothing is labelled because there are no objects to which any surviving subjects could refer in advance. The body as an "unconscious articulation of language", which today serves as a paradigm of visual culture, is, therefore, nothing more than empty visual language and an emptier kind of visual communication. Are that language and that communication something "meaningless"? Certainly, the language and communication in which visuality in the form of visualization stamps the seal of being information are interconnected. In order for a visual language to be able to talk to another, and for visual communication to be a fundamental means of interpersonal relationships, it would be necessary for the world to construct informatics as an essential power regarding the matter of things. Speaking of language and communication as information that is compressed and, moreover, mutually compressed in the space–time period of history leads to the suppression of the dualism of subject and object in the scape of digital reality.

That language, let us say that firmly, becomes *the thing*. The language of the new media might be postponed information without referring to anything other than communication (number), visuality (picture) and body (word). The digital era, therefore, should be based on the "calculated picture", as Friedrich Kittler theoretically observed. This means that the machine-generated picture has determined the very complex of communication in the information or telematics society. The primacy of the number–image over the word is not that the binary (digital) code now allows a new language, but rather that the language itself might be in its articulation a new body of the digital world. However, the body that has been created with the "new world" of machine-generated text combines everything so far separated in the historical sequence of letters, pictures and texts. No doubt there is a radical visualization of the word with which the body connects in interactive communication with another body. The body, therefore, is represented as the incarnation of the word, but not the number or the image. In the fourth book of the New Testament, the gospel of John, the word (*logos*) precedes the number and the picture, because the *logos* as word ontologically allows one and all in the form of visual representation. *In the beginning was the Word (...) And the Word became flesh.*

In its pure numerical representation, the body could be necessarily articulated as a word. It sends a message to other bodies. The closeness of the circle in which the three-member structure of the signifier, the signified and the sign corresponds to the imaginative, symbolic and real constitution of the "meaning" of the contemporary world of the digital age is represented by the closeness of time without the future. The circuit is complete in its capabilities. Therefore, it will be inevitably empty of all other meanings, except for autoreferential and interreferential ones. Symbols circulate without a centre of the circle (Paić 2008: 145–226). Their mutual relationship is mediated by turning the sign into their own emptiness of meaning. We can say that the sign is bent on a mere number, image and word. Indeed, it is the origin of semiotics, Lacanian psychoanalysis and poststructuralism. That "holy triad" of contemporary theory concerning the main issues of culture must be holding the whole postmetaphysical building on its shoulders, and does so pretty well in the traces of Nietzsche, Marx, Kierkegaard and Heidegger.

Whoever wants to talk about "excess meaning" in the visual culture of our age must consequently speak of "lack of meaning". Dreams as an imaginary template of the symbolic construction of reality in the pre-media age still had a trace of the presence of the world in the marking, signing and prediction of future events. However, dreams are now only a sublimated form of "imagining" or a pictorial articulation of possible events in reality. The reality of events precedes dreams in terms of the construction of virtualities. In the film *Minority Report*, the killer is strictly pre-marked. He is detected as the one to kill. That is why it needs to be prevented in advance. But in advance, it signifies what Heidegger in *Being and Time* calls existential Being-to-death. The future is coming up in the form of imaginary precariousness as well as care for an authentic way of the future. What does it really mean to "care" for the future if it is clear today that the technical disposition has itself the power to redefine reality from a desire to a thing, from matter to the possibility of changing state? This seems to be a crucial issue for new approaches to the technical change of life as such and has important ontological implications.

1.4   Conclusion

Who or what escapes from being scared before a terrible event? The living creature in its existence is determined by the primary dimension of the future. It is eccentric, because there is no other organ to deal with in the world except already technologically significant, media-produced tools for survival in nature. The brain and arm are, hence, the spiritual and bodily organs of eccentric existence. Without the brain, the hand does not work. So the body is always thrown into situations in its pre-flight structure. Trying to control them by trying to see them in advance, the body is thrown into the structural timing of what Heidegger calls being-there (*Dasein*; Heidegger 2018: 56–70). Here, of course, the word explicitly enters the human body. The situations are not out of focus and predictably depict the structure of the temporality of the future. This structure encompasses the non-evasive and pre-running features, because any escape from that assemblage seems quite impossible.

The famous movie *The Matrix* (hyper)realistically, imaginatively and symbolically stretches in all directions of the empty past and the future. Why should we emphasize that word—*empty*? Because the structure of the temporality of virtual reality is represented by the simultaneous moment of information. The "here" and "now" are a virtual network of non-identity actors. We no longer have a dream of pictorial predication of future events. The events allow us to be visual, present in dreams as avatar bodies. This is the turn of those ancient Taoist puzzles in the narrative of the philosopher-butterfly Tzuang-Tsi who asked: "Am I Tzuang-Tsi who dreams of being a butterfly or a butterfly who dreams of being Tzuang-Tsi?" The answer is neither in the philosopher nor in the butterfly, but in the realization of dreams as the virtual reality of the world. So the philosopher and the butterfly exist only as immersed images in dreams. *Immersion*, thus, becomes a fundamental feature of the image in the digital age (Flusser 2005; Grau 2003). Moreover, immersion should only be that which is not understood "in space" as it was in the assemblage of traditional metaphysics. Therefore, the body is not immersed in a lively mud or underground unconscious water. Instead, the digitally created body in its immersion can be all and nothing, both the avatar and the real being, the projection of the desire and the creature created from the dream of art. In today's libidinal economy, everything is a subject of desire and nothing is forever determined by its natural origin.

References

Assmann, Aleida. 2008. *Einführung in die Kulturwissenschaft: Grundbegriffe, Themen, Fragestellungen.* 2nd ed. Berlin: Erich Schmidt Verlag.

Baudrillard, Jean. 1991. Ballard's *Crash*. In *Simulacra and Simulation, Two Essays*, translated from French by Arthur B. Evans. [Online] Accessed November 28, 2018. https://www.depauw.edu/sfs/backissues/55/baudrillard55art.htm.

Best, Steven, and Douglas Kellner. 2001. *The Postmodern Adventure: Science, Technology and Cultural Studies at the Third Millennium.* New York and London: The Guilford Press.

Bhabha, Homi K. 1994. *The Location of Culture.* London and New York: Routledge.

Butler, Judith. 1990. *Gender Trouble: Feminism and the Subversion of Identity.* London and New York: Routledge.

———. 1993. *Bodies That Matter.* London and New York: Routledge.

Damasio, Antonio. 2005. *Descartes' Error: Emotion, Reason, and the Human Brain.* New York: Penguin Books.

Debord, Guy. 1994. *The Society of the Spectacle.* Translated from French by Donald Nicholson-Smith. New York: Zone Books.

Featherstone, Mike, and Roger Burrows, eds. 1995. *Cyberspace/Cyberbodies/Cyberpunk: Cultures of Technological Embodiment.* London: SAGE.

Flusser, Vilém. 2005. *Medienkultur*. Frankfurt/M: S. Fischer.

Grau, Oliver. 2003. *Virtual Art: From Illusion to Immersion*. Translated from German by Gloria Custance. Cambridge, MA and London: The MIT Press.

Grosz, Elisabeth. 1994. *Volatile Bodies: Toward a Corporal Feminism*. Bloomington, IN: Indiana University Press.

Heidegger, Martin. 2018. *Sein und Zeit*. GA, Vol. II, 2nd ed. Frankfurt/M: V. Klostermann.

Lacan, Jacques. 1996. *Écrits*. Translated from French by Bruce Fink. London and New York: W.W. Norton & Company.

Mersch, Dieter. 2006. *Medientheorien: Eine Einführung*. Köln: Junius Verlag.

Mitchell, W.J.T. 1987. *Iconology: Image, Text, Ideology*. Chicago: The University of Chicago Press.

Musil, Robert. 1995–1996. *The Man Without Qualities*. Vols. I–II. Translated from German by Burton Pike and Sophie Wilkins. New York: Vintage.

Paić, Žarko. 2006. *A Picture without the World: The Iconoclasm of Contemporary Art*. Zagreb: Litteris.

———. 2007a. *Event and Emptiness: The Essays on the End of History*. Zagreb: Antibarbarus Editions.

———. 2007b. *Fashion Vertigo: Towards a Visual Semiotics of the Body*. Zagreb: Altagama.

———. 2008. *Visual Communication: An Introduction*. Zagreb: Center for Visual Studies.

———. 2011. *Posthuman Condition: The End of Man and Odds of Other History*. Zagreb: Litteris.

Pedraza, Rafael López. 1986. *Anselm Kiefer: "After the Catastrophe"*. London: Thames and Hudson.

Sutlić, Vanja. 1987. *The Practice of Labor as Scientific History: Historical Thinking as Criticism of the Crypto-Philosophical Structure of Marx's Thought*. 2nd ed. Zagreb: Globus.

Welsch, Wolfgang. 1996. *Grenzgänge der Ästhetik*. Stuttgart: Reclamm.

2

The Return to the Body

2.1 Introduction

Let us move in the order of the following axiom: the return to the body denotes one of the ways in which philosophy ends up in its metaphysical destiny of Western history. It might be the event of the "dark nineteenth century", as Heidegger once cryptically said. Just after that, a radical deconstruction of all history really began. In this context we should emphasize that Nietzsche was a thinker who reflected upon the significance of constructing a human taxonomy in a notebook, kept in preparation for *Thus Spoke Zarathustra*, from spring–summer 1883:

> My demand: to produce beings who stand sublimely (*erhaben dastehen*) above the whole human species: and to sacrifice oneself and one's "neighbours" to this goal. (Nietzsche, KSA 10, 7 [21], 2005)

Nevertheless, he decided to turn around the entire metaphysics immersed in the world of ideas without direct relations to the ground and Earth itself, including the passion of the body and its sublime ecstasy. The body that he thinks, feels and suffers takes on the disintegrated

© The Author(s) 2019
Ž. Paić, *White Holes and the Visualization of the Body*,
https://doi.org/10.1007/978-3-030-14467-8_2

metaphysical category. Moving the centre from Heaven to Earth, from beyond or transcendent to immanent, takes place in the entire postmetaphysical view of Marx and Nietzsche to Merleau-Ponty, Derrida, Foucault, Lacan, Baudrillard. However, incorporation is no longer the act of superseding the human above. This can be determined by the freedom of foundation from below. In painting, it happens by moving light from Heaven to Earth. Van Gogh illuminates it openly in the open nature of nature itself. The sky is no longer illuminated. If so, then the Earth itself burns and illuminates the beings. In the poetry of Arthur Rimbaud, at the end of the *Season in Hell*, the advent of "shining cities" was sublimely announced. This prophetic book of absolute modernity ends with these words:

> And I will able to *possess the truth within one soul and one body.* (Rimbaud 1976)

The truth is "possessed" because it is embodied. *A Season in Hell* ends with the keyword of modernity—*body*. If we omit that even Rimbaud in *Illuminations* opens radically new possibilities of speech on the body/text/image, with a distortion of the entire metaphysical framework of Platonism and Christianity between this disclosure of trauma and the greatness of the modern subject, there is only one inevitable question: Who is by any means the subject of possessing "truth" in the equivalence of soul–body? The answer is already given in *The Letters of the Visionary*:

> It is wrong to say: *I think*. One ought to say: *I am thought*. Pardon the pun. I am another. Too bad for the wood if it wakes up as a violin—and screw the rock-brains who prattle on in their ignorance! (Rimbaud 2008: 56)

In the 1960s in his interpretation of Rimbaud's poetry, French-Greek philosopher of the Heideggerian-Marxian direction of thought Kostas Axelos referred to what can be read from the entire poetic work of the founder of modernity. Basically, it is about overcoming/abolishing (*Aufhebung*) the boundaries of the technical planetary world of equivalence in differences by transforming the subject of that ephemeral event (Axelos 1964). The question of the subject in contemporary visual culture remains unquestioned by the fact that the subject is something related to the structure of the self, selfhood, the person. "The darkness of the nineteenth century" completed the idea and concept of the new narrative of the infinite empire of the subject (Zima 2007: 107–153). Hegel, however, speculatively-dialectically performed thinking on the science of absolute spirit by abolishing all the difference in the identity of the substance–subject. For Marx, on the contrary, this encompasses the unity of overcoming/abolishing (*Aufhebung*) the boundaries of capital as a substance–subject of history in the community of direct producers (the realized truth of communism as the beginning of the "new history"). For Nietzsche, the figure of Superman is ruling behind completed history as the eternal return of one and the same, which prevails in the overturning of the previous values, the spirit/soul–body, metaphysics–physics, by surpassing the subject as the mindset of the creator of history. Truth has become a perspective illusion of the object's movement, and the subject could always be just a fiction of a person's identity. Hegel, Marx and Nietzsche thought about the equivalence of substance–subject as *absolute spirit, capital* and *will to power*, whereby Rimbaud, moreover, kept in mind the same way with the different path of his poetry. The subject is neither "strong" nor "weak". It can appear as a problem of the constitution of objects of self-consciousness only after a failed synthesis at the centre of the body itself. Because, as Rimbaud says, that I am someone else and that I do not think, but that they think me, is the only ground for the knowledge of the very essence of the body itself. It was extinguished by the emptiness of all definitions and their ineffectiveness without relying on the superficial in general (Badiou 2008: 68–90). The subject cannot be anything else but the illusion/fiction of the absolute freedom of self and selfhood in the closely surrounding world (*Umwelt*).

Can this argument convince us that this assumption sounds embarrassing to today's revival of the subject from the golden tomb of history? But would it not be paradoxical that they are truly key thinkers of modernity and that a poet who demanded that we "should be absolutely modern" still dominates nowadays with the old dichotomy of subject–object in the nineteenth century? Rimbaud does not talk about "the other me". We cannot assume that thinking, just like the process of "subject" awareness of the stage of its unconscious immersion in nature and the surrounding world, as at the beginning of the world's history with the mythic equivalence of divine and human. Thinking means to be the one who thinks what he really thinks. The Other is not another "subject" nor the Big Other (God or any of the substitute figures). The Other should be constituted as Other only when the possibilities of thinking in the first single person appear in all aspects. That is what I mean, I think exactly like a person; but not as the absolute creator of thoughts, rather with a mediating directness of speech, which constitutes me as an undeniable Other. "Nonsense" is not unarticulated and yet-not-arrived in the stage of self-consciousness about self as the Same and the Other. There are only those who start from the wrong assumption that a human is a warehouse and a maze of the uncanny power of primary impulses and powers.

Who thinks just right about me or "I"? No other, I am not in that beyond myself. In my thinking, as a saying, I dissociate myself from "me" and become someone else by being aware of this process of separation and reunion. The violin is made of wood. But it goes beyond the substantive nature of its objectification (the body of the violin) by its substance–subject art of music. Without a vocalist of music as an artist who serves the object to make music a brilliant experience of exceeding the boundaries of everyday enjoyment in above things, the violin is an aesthetic wooden object. But the violinist is not the "subject" of music. Music as art through the violin by the violinist's skill to produce a composite piece of sound articulation makes sense of the silence and cacophony of the surrounding world.

2.2   Merleau-Ponty—Phenomenology of the Body

In an attempt to meditate on the power and powerlessness of a subject in contemporary visual culture on which Lacanian psychoanalysis is based, among other theoretical orientations, one must proceed from what is available as *an object*. In this way, in the attempt to establish a phenomenological "body philosophy" in postmetaphysical thinking, only one philosopher after Heidegger tried to understand where and why the body belongs and why it is the basis for any future renewal of the narrative of the subject. Of course, this is Maurice Merleau-Ponty and his thinking derived from the book *Phenomenology of Perception*. For Heidegger, the body does not at all appear to be a Being-in-the-world at the level of the understanding of the Being exposed in *Being and Time*. This also applies to the second phase of his thinking after the turn (*die Kehre*). The body lies at the core of thoughts that the Being as an event must be structured within the existential being there (*Dasein*). It is located in the surrounding world (*Umwelt*), but does not have the quality of a thing, much less a "facility", but rather also show that those are manifest only in aspects already placed before as presence-at-hand (*Vorhandenheit*).

A step of consciousness towards understanding the phenomenon should be the turning point in philosophy after the decay of the metaphysics of subjectivity. Inside and out, awareness of the subject of observation is now constituted. The emphasis had been on setting awareness of objects. It is now the turning point that I being a subject in the meaning of what is being shown determines the consciousness of its cognitive-reflective boundary. Heidegger referred to this problem at the seminars he held in Le Thor in France at the end of the 1960s by analysing the concept of the representation of image and body. The first term moves to the position of *ego cogito*. From it comes the possibility of placing objects of consciousness. Subjects think of themselves, setting themselves on the things of consciousness. This should be a step towards the representational theory of the image. Where is the Louvre Museum in Paris? In the head or in the brain? Not in either one or the other. Heidegger suggests that the notion of the Louvre is only possible when the image *re-presents* what appears to be "there". What we see, phenomenologically speaking, is not a picture of the Louvre. What we see comes from the concept of meaning in putting it in front of it. To do this, *aisthesis* might really be needed.

Awakening, thus, should not be a mere aesthetic view of something. On the contrary, observation signifies an act of separation on the subject of what is corporeal, shown in its dual nature of physicality. We should be noting something already mentioned: physicality in an aesthetic sense and corporeality in the sense of the substance of a subject in the living environment encompass the two essential preconditions to observing what the body makes concerning the essential substance–subject of visibility in perception. Pointing to the dangers of the dualism of the body as aesthetic and as substance (*Körper* and *Leib*), Heidegger comes to the essential limit of any phenomenology of physicality. The boundary between one and the Other denotes that the former (aesthetic) somehow belongs to the world as a horizon of meaning, and the latter (actuality) exits from that horizon and even from the surrounding world (*Umwelt*). If we keep this in mind, then the world might only be there when we witness the ways of articulating language in the notion of Being (Heidegger 1977: 58–60).

What does this mean? Is the world at all like a horizon of meaning without language? The reason Heidegger cannot think of the body as an essential problem of thought seems to look into what is crucial for the overall contemplation of visualization. It is an ontological deprivation that the world can think differently than in the essential dimension of language and speech. It can be said that without language there is no world. Or, more accurately, without language there is no picture of the world. Visually impaired language with its substitute syntax, semantics and pragmatics can only be conditional in the "meaning" horizon of the world. When contemporary visual theorist and visual studies co-founder W.J.T. Mitchell asserts that there are no visual media and that for the understanding of digital culture we have produced new *sense relations*, he refers to the problem of overcoming the delineation of language, image and sound in the new paradigm of visual communication (Mitchell 2005). The body is now constituted as a digital image—from being information. So the difference is only that instead of the number (communication) and the image (visual), the body inevitably links itself with the text, the language of which is the basis. In the new world of digital visual technology, the world of the body is a body without a world. How can this be explained? The disappearance of the horizon of the world in language, which is now being transformed into a *thing*, signifies that the body has become an object of an entirely different reality. The problem lies in that we cannot proclaim as just meaningless this and the new digital "world". Quite definitely, other rules of the game should be applying to that. The body as an image or the body as a medium, therefore, determines the new rules of the game.

Merleau-Ponty understands the body phenomenologically, starting from its object structure as a perceived object. So the body is already in advance in the world. It is perceived as an object of consciousness that reflects on itself directed towards the closest one. Husserl's discovery that every consciousness is intentional, that every consciousness is already conscious of something, might be objectified here. The body is not a mere object of perception of consciousness from the position of the transcendental ego. It is a constituent feature of the facility, and of course might be the subject of consciousness in the physiological state of the substance to which the view is directed. The body looks up. But it is at the same time structured just like the other one of consciousness. The view comes from the body and the body is constituted with a view. In Lacan's *XI seminar* entitled "The Four Fundamental Concepts of Psychoanalysis", the gaze, which simultaneously constitutes the subject, starts from the object of lust or the unconscious. Merleau-Ponty in his posthumously published book *Visible and Invisible* is placed in the horizon of discernment beyond visual phenomenology (Lacan 2004). The problem lies in the fact that Lacan, in agreement with Merleau-Ponty, is, basically, on the focal point of overcoming the possibility of speaking about what builds on other foundations, unlike Descartes and the modern philosophy of subjectivity—the psychoanalytic theory of the subject.

While Merleau-Ponty starts with pathological forms of perception to get insight into the object's bodily structure, and we see that Baudrillard also speaks of the end of the body in the visual fascination with "holes" and fragmented organs without a body, on the other hand Lacan approaches the problem as the object of desire from the perspective of what is identical to the contemporary visualization. We can see that the problem of the relationship between perception, visuality and fantasy lies in the midst of a reconsideration concerning mind–body metaphysics.[1] Who is actually watching and who is being watched? Does it look and see the body only among other bodies, or is it an illusory view without which consciousness cannot at any time possess its inner and outer existence? In all three cases, bodily reflection should be determined by inevitable talk of the subject and the object of seeing. However, visualization is obviously more than the aesthetic dimension of understanding the world. It is related to perception, and perception with the cognitive ability to observe. Thinking is not visual, but visuality has an important dimension of thinking that imagines (visualizes) concepts.

When Lacan says that unconsciousness is articulated as a language, from the tradition of Freudian psychoanalysis he points to the "dark" dimension of thought. But the unconscious is precisely *what* we are thinking when language occurs as the presence/absence of Being in language. *What* articulated as a language might be, therefore, the thinking that goes beyond its so-called unconscious mode of Being. The view is visually inaccessible. Consciousness, however, in the modern era deserves the dignity of a new concept for being thoughtful beings. Only humans have awareness of themselves because they have the ability to reflect on their own body as the centre of their relationship to the world. Consciousness for Descartes was an essential feature of the ability of thought as a substance that places itself in the position of the subject of thought. I think therefore I am (*cogito ergo sum*). This *cogito* assumes the reflexive or pre-existing condition which always constitutes language in the knowledge of what it is (*quidditas*).

Therefore, the entirety of contemporary philosophy is not without reason called the *metaphysics of light*. All its concepts were an attempt to illuminate the creature in an area of the visible. But visualizing concepts that go beyond the empirical phenomenon of God, Being, time and event is always just marking and tracing something beyond the visible. The language should be precisely *that* or the "thing of thought". When language is rotten to the level of the organs, a pure instrument of communication, the media, it is transformed into a *thing*. We can see that the pronunciation of the language exceeds the instrumental speaking function. The information is not preceded by the meaning of the message being expressed through language. Quite the contrary, language brings information up to the higher degree of the articulated message as a guide to action. It is therefore determined that language expresses what is relevant to the world only when it is assembled in speech. However, the language of the new media cannot absorb the mystical, technical-technological information processing in the digital code (Manovich 2001).

It is a language that expresses the new talk of technology and culture. Knowing its syntax, semantics and pragmatics means being immersed in the assemblage of visual communication. The body, therefore, appears in the context of the digital "world" as:

1. language,
2. speech, and
3. the thing of a technology-generated thinking machine (computer as apparatus).

The body as a language could be articulated by the symbolic system of the sign, the signifier and the signified. No doubt, we are facing the fundamentals of visual semiotics. Many voices from the current paradigm shift in the field of visual studies and image science are trying to establish quite a new attempt to analyse the assemblage of visualization and the body. Among them, this new semiotics has taken a very good position thanks to its applicable terms, which could be advance know-how for case studies related to disciplines beyond the boundaries of the humanities and social sciences. Body language, therefore, cannot be a purely gestural language. Right there we are experiencing a condition of possibilities by which the body enters the markings of its identity and the difference with other bodies. The body's speech, in turn, involves a complex syntax, semantics and pragmatics of visual bodily design in general. Gestures and mimicry, decoration, digestion, intervention, surgery, implantation change the natural bodily structure into the cultural metamorphosis of its many new forms. Indeed, the body as matter never signified something radically opposed to its language and speech. Moreover, matter is shown by the technical-technological processing of language and body language. It can be argued that matter in the sense of a technologically determined body decides on a new language and body language.[2]

Only then can it be constituted as a "desiring machine" (Deleuze and Guattari). Thinking and lust—*res cogitans and res extensa* in the new dualism of the body from its immanent structure of the object—are no longer *abandoned* as abruptly as in the previous age of modern metaphysics. The barefoot and "white holes" of the body in its objectification and postmetaphysical flow point to the uncanny power of synthesis. From that perspective, the problem might be ontological and encompasses the cognitive-epistemological turn. How can the *immanence* of events still speak about the one behind or beyond the body itself (Günzel 1998)? This question will be discussed in detail in the interpretation of Deleuze's thinking on the body without organs by the light of the basic assumptions about the body as visual fascination. Let us say that the immanence of the body, not the consciousness, represented the only deconstructive path of the subject's development through the psychoanalytic concept of the unconscious to the concept of the new subject as a *rhizome*. The subject, however, is neither body nor consciousness. Therefore, the unconscious articulation of the language by which a technologically advanced body opens up to the new technological environment or the surrounding world of objects creates that new or decentered subject (Lacan). To say that such a thing involves the incarnation of consciousness implies an unconscious articulation of language.

Let us recall Merleau-Ponty's attempt to return to the phenomenological body, which it had shared from the very beginning of Western metaphysics. The paradox appears to be an approach to the body as an object, an external subject, something outside the act of observing consciousness. In a physiological sense, the body cannot be anything but an object available to all other activities of mind, spirit, soul. From that viewpoint, what we are now directly perceiving is that is not the way of the phenomenological structure of the "body idea". We wonder how Merleau-Ponty comprehended the relationship between consciousness, the unconscious and the body in sexuality. It is well known that for Sartre in *Being and Nothingness*, the problems of the body, the gaze and the Other were asserted from the horizon of creating a new existential psychoanalysis. Contrary to Freud, Sartre's analysis of imagination and the imaginary came to criticize Husserl's transcendental subject. Freud, for the authenticity of existence in the universe of social relations, was only a methodological starting point. But every psychology that operates with the unconscious notion of phenomenology and the philosophy of existence was deprived of the cognition of being a subject at all. It is not necessarily the foundation of the subject in that understanding, but rather a negative possibility of self-existence in the mode of consciousness about its essence.

Merleau-Ponty has been in the path of phenomenology and Heidegger's thoughts from the time of the destruction of traditional ontology in *Being and Time*, when he came to the realization that the unconscious in

Freud's sexuality and the psychoanalysis that won the new field of contemporary culture research is not at all an ontological problem of consciousness. In other words, instead of enframing the essence of sexuality and the body as an object in the unconscious production of phantasms, we must begin by saying that sexuality is

> not the even transcendent in human life or in its centre presented by unconscious concepts. It is constantly present in it as an atmosphere. (Merleau-Ponty 2014: 183)

The body as the sexual object of the desire of the Other is only one of the modes of presence/absence of the body of the Other. The subject is not, therefore, the one who sets the object by the act of constructing consciousness about it. Both objects as an object of lust and an entity as a consciousness of desire that arises from the facility are only made possible by transcending sexuality into what Merleau-Ponty calls the *more general drama of life*. Bodily experience surpasses sexuality as an atmosphere. This experience is represented an existential drama of transcending life from that "hole in being"—Sartre's expression from *Being and the Nothingness* took over from Hegel—in which a human is placed in apparent confrontation with the limits of every physical experience.

The body in its overshoots of "natural" boundaries faces resistance within the sphere of sexuality. But sexuality is by no means merely an uncanny urge to die as the final border of the body. Merleau-Ponty, as well as Lacan, takes the mirror figure in a Platonic sense to show the inner connection from perception, body and sexuality to Being overall. Similar to Lacan, who said that the subject constitutes the gaze looking at the Other, for Merleau-Ponty's thinking, a mirror appears as the self-assertion of existence in the visual field of human perception. What is here decisive to our analysis of the body's disappearance in the visualization of contemporary media culture? The critique of psychoanalysis undertaken by Merleau-Ponty derives from the significant difference between the phenomenological notion of the world and Lacan's psychoanalytic comprehension of the construction of the subject as a decentered field of the unconscious articulation of language. Sexuality represented a keyword to psychoanalysis in research on the archipelago and labyrinth of unconscious projections of desire in all forms of bodily expression. Merleau-Ponty, hence, does not deny the significance of sexuality in order to comprehend the body. In any case, he carries out a completely different way of thinking.[3] Sexuality, therefore, is not closed, but neither does it raise the question of the existential-ontological assemblage of the body in the world.

Bodily boundaries are not the limits of language, as the limits of sexuality are not the limits of the subject. How could we correctly comprehend this assumption? It is well known that Wittgenstein in his concept of language games has come to the key setting for any future philosophy of language. His view that the limits of my language are the limits of my world corresponds to Heidegger's issues, dated from the time of the destruction of traditional ontology in *Being and Time*, as a true horizon of the meaning of Being (Romp 2006). In that matter, the essence of the world might be the passage of being there (*Dasein*) in the way of existential Being-to-death. It should also be noted that language in its essence could show the true openness of the world. So the horizon of the meaning of the world is determined by language, and thinking is being expressed as words in the assemblage of meaning. We speak the language of the world in the matrix of the primordial or *pre-language* (*Ur-Sprache*), but not as subjects that construct objects; rather, as rulers and those who are "there" in order for the world to speak of its worldliness in the historical mark of the epoch.

When we say that the limits of the body are not the limits of language, then it is primarily thought that the corporeality of the body is not the same thing as the worldliness of the world. The world does not inhabit only bodies. If that were so, we could have the whole art, for example, of Francis Bacon in his research on the "flesh" of the body reduced to the language of the body exhausted in the self-teaching of the somatic without semiotics. The body has its limits, in that it can only be opened to the world as a language that has lost the essence of being spoken and moved to speak *things*. In this way, the boundaries of sexuality, which rests on the desire for an object beyond my body, are not the limits of a subject, because the term "the subject" is now derived from the very constitution of the body itself. It is an ontological illusion that necessarily rests on Lacan's psychoanalysis to be able to speak of an unconscious and lust at all.

The body represented an ontological "scandal" for the whole of metaphysics. This must also be emphasized, because it is not talk about the so-called problems of materialism and idealism. Without any kind of doubt, the body does not have a substance. However, it cannot be proof of the materialistic theory of knowledge as opposed to idealism based on the primacy of ideas and spirit. Embodiment goes beyond both "visionary" concepts. In an attempt for the body to appear in the world at all, it has to be embodied. The difference between the essentialism of the spirit and the existential one-sidedness of the body is that for traditional metaphysics the body is an embodiment of the spirit, and for the postmetaphysical view of Nietzsche to Deleuze, the body is represented as an imminent embodiment of its own being. It should be neither the mere fact nor the mere spiritual one. The converse of "being" the body as *essence* is obviously not just talking about being a human. Moreover, the body cannot only be anthropologically determined by the human body. This has been the focus of recent studies focusing on the analysis of human, animal and cyborg (Haraway 2008). So the body's corporeality does not run out of being a human. The assumption for the entire turning of philosophy as metaphysics in thinking on the body was undoubtedly the psychoanalysis of Freud on the trajectory of Nietzsche. In the philosophical sense, the beginning is related to Heidegger and the existential analytic of being there (*Dasein*). The philosophy of existence in its reversal of the metaphysical scheme that the essence of existence (the *fact* that *there* is something original at first) precedes being, at the height of Sartre's existentialism, signified the birthplace of the physical body. We could note, therefore, that the body lies in the *corporeal turn*, which begins with Lacan's psychoanalysis and Deleuze's philosophical decentered subject in the late 1960s, and assumes an understanding of the essential existence of the freedom of unconscious articulation of the subject through language. *It* is no longer above or behind the body. *It* is in the body itself. What we call *that* matters in contemporary philosophy, it takes the form of the transcendental matrix related to bodily existence in the empirical world of multitudinous phenomena.

To psychoanalysis as well as to phenomenology, it is primarily an "object" that derives from the world's worldliness, and its subjectivity gains its view (*regard*). The subject, apparently paradoxically, constitutes the view of the Other. Already at the very beginning of the modern art of deconstruction of the body, we are faced with the assumption that in the infallible, intuitive way expressed by Paul Klee is how exactly subjects are being perceived by objects.

The visual grammar of the body in this sense precedes the syntax and the pragmatism of sexuality. On Heidegger's trajectory, but also in critical deflection, Merleau-Ponty's merit was to open the possible horizon that the body is trying to understand the world's worldliness as a language of the visibility and invisibility of the world itself. Not a single phenomenon is closed to itself. So sexuality cannot be reduced to the unconscious, even when it is mediated by cultural (symbolic) worlds of meaning during its historical development. The exit from the vicious circle of Heidegger's thinking on the subject has been shown in the destruction of two concepts—the consciousness and the world. It is simultaneously an open path of surmounting the closed structure of the contemporary body as a visual fascination. In addition, the following must be said: consciousness and the body should not be separated in the traditional way, as was inherent in modern rationalism on Descartes' path. By contrast, the body becomes conscious of its own movements and feelings, starting not from consciousness outside the world, but rather from its world, as the language allows for existence in the form of the absolute I and its pre-reflexive derivatives. As mentioned earlier, we have to see the hidden beginning of the *corporeal turn*.

Consciousness and unconsciousness derive the novel structures of the subject. The world in its essential sense of the openness of the horizon is shown in the medium of language. Its transformation into the *thing* that precedes the realities of visual fascination stems from the technical construction of the world. Understanding how and why the body does not exist without language as the horizons of the world means opening up the question of the relationship between language and things. In another context, this seems very significant regarding the ontological-phenomenological question about the world and the body. It is not quite outside the topic that Heidegger points to what belongs to things in the surrounding world (*Umwelt*). Things are quite different from objects because they are here already, they are not produced in a technical way. For this reason, we must always be aware of the differences and boundaries between the original understanding of Being and the modern reduction of thinking on scientific-technical setting/enframing. So the body lies in the midst of the event of the openness of Being and time, including the surrounding world. To the relevant world to language and things as a surrounding world, it can obviously only be thought of as "set" in the gap between language and things. The body might be, therefore, always *between-being* (*inter-esse*). Being between two—language and thing— means to be acting-in-between. What can today in visual communication be called imperative—namely, the interactive communication of networked subjects/actors of information exchange and the creation of new events—could be media activity *between* the networked bodies. Activity is only active when it occurs in space–time's physical presence among other objects (Lovejoy 2004: 220–269). Interactive action, hence, is the opposite to the inter-personality of communication participants. This is the result of the implosion (compression and summarizing) of information and the communication explosion. The contemporary body should be strictly located between these two binary members of the logic of the digital age. Its communication ecstasy might be the result of the disappearance of the difference between language and things, technology and culture. When everything overlaps, it passes from one form to another. Only a body has metamorphic qualities from its eccentric position in the world in fractal light sources. McLuhan already said that electricity as a condition of modern media capabilities is represented by the decentralized space–time of physical disappearance in pure information (McLuhan 2018).[4]

Being between languages and things does not mean being between two separate "worlds". The body reconciles opposites, binary oppositions, paradoxes and contradictions. Only with the openness of the world in which the body interactively acts should the encounter of the body in space–time reach a state of feasibility. Indeed, the language of the contemporary body designates the "thing" of the body's thinking as a medium or an image. In other words, what the body articulates as the *one* on the other side of language is the other side of the thing. Being and

Being-beyond are just two ways of Being-in-the-world. The body floats in the emptiness of its own abandonment from Heaven and its own unrivalled news on Earth. In a 1950 lecture entitled "The Thing" (*Das Ding*), Heidegger established a fourfold of the Earth and the sky, the divine and the mortal. Their fourfold lines determine what we call the world. But these fourfold lines throughout the history of metaphysics do not cast light on how it is possible at the end of history to equalize the world with the surrounding world (*Umwelt*), or whether the entire horizon of the world's meaning will be the very fact that the surrounding world becomes the only one of all possible worlds. What bestows the openness to the Earth and the sky, divine and mortal fourfold should be the original free bond of mirror play. Thus, the language and the world and the thing are all held only within the free connection of the fourfold that derives from this unrestrained freedom of the mirroring game:

> Earth and sky, divinities and mortals—being at one with one another of their own accord—belong together by way of the simpleness of the united fourfold. Each of the four mirrors in its own way the presence of the others. Each therewith reflects itself in its own way into its own, within the simpleness of the four. This mirroring does not portray a likeness. The mirroring, lightening each of the four, appropriates their own presencing into simple belonging to one another. Mirroring in this appropriating-lightening way, each of the four plays to each of the others. The appropriative mirroring sets each of the four free into its own, but it binds these free ones into the simplicity of their essential being toward one another. (…) Men alone, as mortals, by dwelling attain to the world as world. Only what conjoins itself out of world becomes a thing. (Heidegger 1971: 177, 180)

As the language for visual communication in the digital age becomes interactive, the same happens in the *language of the new media* as a mental image that no longer precedes speech. The pre-emptive, transcendental distinction of empirical disappearance when a *corporeal turn* occurs goes further. Then it is no longer a matter of precedence, of the word to the picture or the image to the words. Thought images are "astral bodies", one stream of the body in the openness of the world. But humans do not produce pictures. The world as language and as matter happens in the pictorial representation of language-things. The human is neither the master of the image, nor the "subject" nor "object" of thought (Belting 2001).

2.3   Conclusion

Ego cogito, the act of founding contemporary thinking on a subject—namely, that "I think" that must follow all my ideas and all my states of involvement in the cognitive process of the external and inner world (opinions)—is not deconstructed by the machine to get something below this grounding act. Lust or the unconscious in the field of construction of a subject that enables the personality of a person is nothing more than what is already present in philosophy following Heidegger (Sartre, Merleau-Ponty, Lacan, Deleuze) as an act of pre-reflexive *cogito*. This direction of thinking that developed with Merleau-Ponty at the periphery of the phenomenology of perception leads us to the fundamental question of this consideration: Why is the visualization of the body as a visual fascination in this media age releasing any connection to transcendental sexuality (obscenity, eroticism, pornography) and relating only to the emptiness of visual communication? To try to give an answer to this question, let us first show what the problem looks like with the revival of Lacan's psychoanalytic theory of the decentered subject and Deleuze's philosophy of the immanence of bodies without organs in the interpretation of the visual "postmetaphysics" of the world. Why is the account of the resurrection or the return of the subject not a sign of the royal power of the "subject", but just the opposite, its total inability to contend with the radical disappearance of the body regarding a picture or a body as a medium in the total transparency of the world in a pure form of spectacle—an event of *things*?

Notes

1. "I mean, and Maurice Merleau-Ponty points this out, that we are beings who are looked at, in the spectacle of the world. That which makes us consciousness institutes us by the same token as speculum mundi. Is there

no satisfaction in being under that gaze of which, following Merleau-Ponty, I spoke just now, that gaze that circumscribes us, and which in the first instance makes us beings who are looked at, but without showing this? The spectacle of the world, in this sense, appears to us as all-seeing. This is the phantasy to be found in the Platonic perspective of an absolute being to whom is transferred the quality of being all-seeing" (Lacan 2004: 74–75).

2. "Sophisticated digital image processing technology, *morphing*, creates conditions for permanent body transformation. Moreover, it creates an entire range of *frames* that allow for a continuous transition from an image of a body to the image of any other body. Examples of using *morphing* *have been* found not only in research within video art but also within mass imaginaries. (…) *Cyberpunk* reduces the importance of the body, though it seems to want to be prominent because it revives the old dream of modernity to free a man from the will of death, emphasizing the body with the help of machines. This means that human beings are also being entangled in being a machine and being *cyber* the body is completely human and artificial" (Codeluppi 2006: 119, 122).

3. Merleau-Ponty understood sexuality in this way: "There is no surpassing of sexuality as there is no sexuality enclosed in oneself" (Merleau-Ponty 2014: 186).

4. The radical continuation of the lumino-kinetic theory of the disappearance of the body in visual fascination is found in the writings of Paul Virilio. The terms of speed, light and information replace traditional metaphysical categories of Being as *energeia* (Aristotle), time as motion in a linear sequence, and space as transcendental dawn. In one essay, Virilio speaks of the disappearance of sexuality and the transformation of the body into a bioplastic flow of exchange of information as an exchange of no more symbolic bodies than virtual–real: "*Together with the* build-up of information superhighways, we are facing a new phenomenon: loss of orientation. A fundamental loss of orientation complementing and concluding the societal liberalization and the deregulation of financial markets whose nefarious effects are well-known. A duplication of sensible reality, into reality and virtuality, is in the making. A stereo-reality of sorts threatens. A total loss of the bearings of the individual looms large. To exist is to exist in situ, here and now, *hic et nunc*. This is precisely what is being threatened by cyberspace and instantaneous, globalized information flows. *What lies ahead* is a disturbance in the perception of what

reality is; it is a shock, a mental concussion. And this outcome ought to interest us. Why? Because never has any progress in a technique been achieved without addressing its specific negative aspects. The specific negative aspect of these information superhighways is precisely this loss of orientation regarding alterity (the other), this disturbance in the relationship with the other and with the world. It is obvious that this loss of orientation, this non-situation, is going to usher a deep crisis which will affect society and hence, democracy" (Virilio 1995).

References

Axelos, Kostas. 1964. *Vers la pensée planétaire*. Paris: Les Éditions de Minuit.

Badiou, Alain. 2008. Rimbaud's Method: Interruption. In *Conditions*, translated from French by Steve Corcoran, 68–90. London and New York: Continuum.

Belting, Hans. 2001. *Bild-Anthropologie: Enwurf für eine Bildwissenschaft*. W. Fink. Munich.

Codeluppi, Vanni. 2006. Liquid Body: The Fashion Behind Narcissism. *Fort* 1–2: 119–122. (Translated from Italian to Croatian by Mirna Cvitan Černelić).

Günzel, Stephen. 1998. *Immanenz: Zum Philosophiebegriff von Gilles Deleuze*. Essen: Blau Eule.

Haraway, Donna J. 2008. *When Species Meet*. Minneapolis and London: University of Minnesota Press.

Heidegger, Martin. 1971. The Thing. In *Poetry, Language, Thought*, translated from German by Alfred Hofstadter. New York: Harper & Row.

———. 1977. *Vier Seminare*. Frankfurt/M: V. Klostermann.

Lacan, Jacques. 2004. *The Four Fundamental Concepts of Psychoanalysis*. Translated from French by Alan Sheridan. London and New York: Routledge.

Lovejoy, Margot. 2004. *Digital Currents: Art in the Electronic Age*. London and New York: Routledge.

Manovich, Lev. 2001. *The Language of New Media*. Cambridge, MA and London: The MIT Press.

McLuhan, Marshall. 2018. *Understanding the Media: The Extensions of Man*. Cambridge, MA and London: The MIT Press.

Merleau-Ponty, Maurice. 2014. *Phenomenology of Perception*. Translated from French by Donald A. Landes. London and New York: Routledge.

Mitchell, W.J.T. 2005. *What Do Pictures Want? The Lives of Loves of Images.* Chicago: Chicago University Press.

Nietzsche, W. Friedrich. 2005. *Nachgelassene Fragmente 1882–1884. Sämtliche Werke. Kritische Studienausgabe.* Berlin: W. de Gruyter.

Rimbaud, Arthur. 1976. *A Season in Hell.* Translated from French by Paul Schmidt. New York: Harper & Row. [Online] Accessed November 12, 2018. http://www.mag4.net/Rimbaud/poesies/Farewell.html.

———. 2008. The Letters of the Visionary. In *Complete Works*, translated from French by Paul Schmidt. New York: Harper.

Romp, Georg. 2006. *Heideggers Philosophie: Eine Einführung.* Wiesbaden: Marixverlag.

Virilio, Paul. 1995. Speed and Information: Cyberspace Alarm! [Online] Accessed November 14, 2018. https://journals.uvic.ca/index.php/ctheory/article/view/14657/5523.

Zima, Peter V. 2007. *Theorie des Subjekts: Subjektivität und Identität Zwischen Modern und Postmodern.* 2nd ed. Tübingen und Basel: A. Francke.

3

The New Theory of the Subject

3.1 Introduction

When Lacan states that "Here man isn't master in his own house" (Lacan 1991: 307), isn't that actually a criticism of modern subjectivity? Why, then, is he still talking about the subject, if not to return to what appears to him to belong to him—to re-master his house? How does lordship or rule stand on the fundamentals of identity, with the support of my own in the world, whether it is paradoxical to require a new concept of subjectivity and to claim that the "master" has to be subordinate (to God?)? And what about self-sacrifice? Lacan's concept of the subject is the individual subject.[1] At the same time, the subject appears to be subordinated and fragmented between something. Obviously, this could already be a problem in the establishment of a new subjectivity of man. But this individual entity cannot be a person in the modern sense of the word. Rather, we can assume that it is a subject in the structural sense of something that should be essential to the novel power of de-subjecting man as master of his own consciousness. In accordance with the poststructuralist deconstruction of the idea of the centre, origin, purity, the discourse of the

© The Author(s) 2019
Ž. Paić, *White Holes and the Visualization of the Body*,
https://doi.org/10.1007/978-3-030-14467-8_3

correctness of the metaphysical order, Lacan named it the decentered subject—*sujet décentré* (Lacan 2004: 164).

Determined to reflect on what is subordinated to something which is itself, a structural analysis of language becomes a fragmented one. The suspicion of being able to express the subject in the terms and categories of the entire historical metaphysics of the language makes Lacan's psycho-analytic method a kind of deconstruction of the power of language in the constitution of the subject's world at large. To be subordinated and to be scattered in itself—as if it were a paradoxical and contradictory act of inability to act beyond the medium of language in the body. Lacan's thinking is the psychoanalytic de-structuring of the subject in the sym-bolic order of language. Why are we talking about the paradoxical and contradictory definition of a subject? One of the reasons might be that such a construction simply represents a radical difference to the novel concept of the subject concerning Descartes and Kant. The *ego cogito* in the former and the transcendental subject of the thinking of the latter are not subordinated to anyone other than themselves and in themselves are *subiectum* to any possible "objectivity" of the outside world.

In order for the subject in its decentered position to be what it is, it must articulate itself through language as it is, unconsciously. Thus, the decentered subject might not be understandable in the causal model (cause–effect). The unconscious articulated as language and the essence of such a subject does not happen anywhere in the world. What is the concept of the world that Lacan assumes? Obviously, no objective corre-lation of consciousness in its unconscious mode can be left intact by the act of deconstruction, which must be complete or remain merely on the horizon of the universe of the individual. The world as a condition of the possibility of appearing to a decentered subject necessarily has to be a decentralized world, or a world that is, in its horizon, meaningful to a subordinated and fragmented subject. Such a world or one in advance (transcendental) rests in a frozen state between the absolute certainty of language and the stuff of experience that creates the position of the sub-ject as *ego cogito* and doubts about the possibility of further understanding on the same foundations as what is being shown as a new house of subjectivity.

Certainty and suspicion are the essential features of the subject in its own foundations. The suspicion raises the certainty of what I think. So the second position is no longer a question of methodology, but a suspicion of the meaning of building a new world as a horizon of meaning without the radical deconstruction of language. Between these two positions, Cartesian and Lacanian, the defence of the quest for the decentered subject, conducted by Slavoj Žižek in a politicized neo-Marxist concept, tries to elaborate on the fundamental view of Heidegger that the narrative of subjectivity is only the consequence of the nihilism of the technical world (Žižek 2000: 9–69, 2006a: 272–329).

Attempting to radicalize Lacan, who admittedly acknowledged that Heidegger's analysis and concepts were accepted in his psychoanalytic theories of the subject, Žižek's thinking finally came to a great return to Descartes and Hegel against Heidegger. However, nihilism cannot be the atmosphere in which the subject is condensed and evaporated, but rather the essence of the modern world of technology. Acting against nihilism might not be returning to the position of a contemporary subject. Moreover, such political action and social engagement without the total "revolution" of being the world signified simply the lack of great expectations and the fall into the abyss of the subjectivism of new values. The ultimate result seems to be that, in the neo-Marxist analysis of global capitalism, it is always an effort to break the concept of ideology with a little help from the ethical-political demands of the radical revolution. Indeed, but what kind of absolute utopian achievement—the transformation of society or the world—has to be made? The ethical problem undoubtedly arises when it comes to the values, postulates, utopias, oppositions and contradictions of society–culture–life. In the background of this rotation in the same enchanting circle lies only the one and the same totally helpless subject in all his modern and postmodern versions in front of the absolute figure of capital as science–technology–things. Capital in its global existence could be exactly a realized substance–subject. After Marx and Nietzsche, and especially after Heidegger and his turn of thought, talk of returning to the subject cannot mean anything other than falling below the level of Hegel's constructive dialectics. Was it necessary to go through this hermeneutic cycle to find ourselves again in the futile development and progress of history as a (new) type of metaphysics?

The problem, therefore, is not a radical change in the world, which governs capital as the subject–substance of the end of the history of the global spectacle of ideology without a visible centre of power, but that every new theory of subjectivity is inevitably repeated; let us say, with Lenin, the "childish disease" of the political subjectivism of modernity. Namely, there is always going to be a *revival* of the social revolution of the world, which has already been revolutionized in its essence by being an absolutely scientific and technical image of the world itself. In Lacanian terms, the world is a real fantasy of imaginary-symbolic production for the production of the purpose of *jouissance* without the substance-pure emptying of the subject in its "white holes".

The world's revolution is impossible for the simple reason that such a world has long been decentralized. If such is the subject of which Lacan speaks, with no substance, what might be the result of the impotence of the empty signifier circle? Society as an unconscious, culture as an unconscious, life in biopolitical production as an unconscious? All social revolutions are nihilistic because the idea of change is derived from what is just the result of modern subjectivity—society. In the late 1960s, Heidegger defined the notion of society beyond to the opposition of civil and industrial society as follows:

> It is just another name or mirror or the extension of subjectivity. (Heidegger 1977: 359)

As a matter of fact, this results in the construction of the world as an "objective" world or a world of scientific and technical production. Its appearance is represented by a consumer capitalist society. This is, in essence, a nihilistic world of infinite emanation. In it, the subject rests on the fiction and the illusion of one's own identity. All contemporary sociological studies of lifestyles and identities speak of that matter and nothing else (Lipovetsky 2006). So it seems completely unclear what is about the so-called collective subject. Even Žižek, on the trail of Badiou, forgets to mention who is really the one who has already been floating in the surrounding world (*Umwelt*) on the foundations of the destruction of traditional ontology, and concludes that the world as a horizon of mean-ing is questioned by its emptiness in the stability of change in the soci-ety–culture of global biopolitical production. The one who is touched or removed in a speech about the emptied world without the horizon of meaning is none other than Heidegger. If we do not live in the world anymore, then its "substance" is something as transparent as societies that crumble into debris by globalizing in the emptiness of communication networks. On the tiresome pseudo-Marxist question of who is subject of the revolution of the world, the answer should be in advance paradoxical as well as necessary. This is not a global proletariat who aspires to become a global new bourgeoisie so that its wealth is generalized to all members of society, but rather a spectacular form of what could be named the "sublime object of ideology"—capital itself. It is already overtaking the social relations revolutionizing the same. The forces of production (capi-tal as science–technology–life) change social relationships, not vice versa. The Real changes the imaginary-symbolic order of discourse and not vice versa. Society is, therefore, a decentralized collective subject, who "is not a master in his own house". Is there anyone else who mastered that house or is it abandoned and empty?

3.2   Lacan's Psychoanalysis

Let us go back to the "centre" of this debate. Why can psychoanalysis no longer be a valid interpretation of what happens when the body disap-pears in pure fascination with the image? In order to approach the answer to that question, we will stop for a while at the very beginning. Lacan did not point out in his subject's analysis that he thinks that psychoanalysis should become an addiction or a theoretical method and an analysis of "new philosophy". In the already mentioned piece from the *XI Seminar* on the gaze and *speculum mundi* in which we talk about being "seen in the theatre of the world", before going into the theory of the picture, Lacan fiddles with the great pretensions of his discipline:

> Psycho-analysis is neither a Weltanschauung nor a philosophy that claims
> to provide the key to the universe. It is governed by a particular aim, which

is historically defined by the elaboration of the notion of the subject. It poses this notion in a new way, by leading the subject back to his signifying dependence. (Lacan 2004: 77)

This strategy of elaborating the philosophical concept of a subject may seem like a sophisticated game. Despite the modesty and inexpressiveness of one's own ideas, in one part of this *XI Seminar* in the understanding of the main idea of its thinking—the Real—Lacan comes to the "ontological" assumption of the overall intention of psychoanalysis. At the end of philosophy, theoretical psychoanalysis intends to become the authorized representative of the interpretation of a "new" subject, with a request for the interpretation of contemporary culture and society as the foundation in a decentralized world. In removing the psychoanalysis of idealism, but also of materialism and realism, Lacan seeks to reach the core of the Real. He comes to this by critically discussing the idea of reducing the experience of social and cultural struggles, classes and human exploitation to the ontology of aspiration. Since psychoanalysis does not result from the notion that life is a dream, but that life is the scene of dream and imagination, the symbolic and real creation of the subject, then it is turning to a real methodological starting point for a completely new epistemological origin. There is, of course, no idealistic or materialistic basis. The subject becomes an experiential field of realism that opens in the close encounter. Using Aristotle's term *empty automaton*, Lacan realistically defines it as beyond the principle of pleasure. It lies behind the *automaton*:

> What is repeated, in fact, is always something that occurs—the expression tells us quite a lot about its relation to the tyché—as by chance. (Lacan 2004: 54)

It is, therefore, the Real which we have to meet to confront the gap between perception and consciousness. The real experience might be shown primarily in some traumatic experience. This notion of reality, it seems, cannot be derived from Kant's modality categories: possible, real (actual), necessary. Real or actual does not translate as reality. It does not apply to material or ideal reality. It could be a meeting of a subject with some sort of racing event in the very core of the Real. The Real, therefore, it is not reality constituting itself, but it witnesses the meeting of the subject in the perception and awareness of something traumatic from the "world". The problem is that it is real on that side. It might not, therefore, be true on the side of the beyond (transcendent). In the tradition of metaphysics, that place is occupied by God. In the notion of real existence, there exists a particular kind of transcendence in the sense of the transcendental form of appearing like something. It is not transcendental lightning or the subject that, like God or Father/Law, manages history, even though Lacan himself is far from an atheistic denial of God's existence (Žižek 1992). The problem is obvious that such a concept of the Real can only be gained from the decentered subjectivity that starts from primary pre-reflexive cognitive activity. No doubt, it must be unconsciously articulated as a language. We constantly recognize unconsciously the puzzle of Freud and Lacan's psychoanalysis. It is at the same time the fundamental concept underlying the new concept of the subject and its identity, but also the fundamental notion with which the entire contemporary visual culture works, without asking about its origins and sources. Can we imagine today the interpretation of a film such as David Lynch's *Blue Velvet* or Paul Anderson's *Magnolia* without that magical interpretative key—the "dark night of the unconscious" (Paić 2007: 147–164)?

The Real as a meeting with the traumatic at the same time carries what is on the surface of the matter, but it is not the only thing to be said. On the other hand, the pleasure principle could not be a transcendental subject or Husserl's consciousness that is always directed (*intentio*) on something as something. It is more real than imaginary and symbolic, because it is not just their "realization" in the lack of one or the other. Therefore, life is not a dream; rather, it is manifested as a dream come true. The Real in the transcendental sense precedes the whole. So we should not be able to understand this temporally and logically-historically, but rather exactly in a strict structural manner. That is the reason why Lacan expresses perhaps the most radical thought of his psychoanalysis. This thought, as it shows, strives to be a substitute for philosophy as the "key to the universe". But unlike traditional metaphysics as ontology, this universe moves to the subject level in the new body discourse, which is defined in its body by the unconscious production of desire, impulse and necessity. The universe on which the word is now small is an anthropological horizon of the world. It replaced the "great big universe". So this "new" universe should be called the universe of scattered "souls". And the "soul" is reduced to the primary structure of the libidinal economy. "The key to the universe", which in the ironical but extremely radical turn of Nietzsche's assumption was quite wrongly taken with the mark of atheism, as also Lacan takes it in fact without serious analysis, is the next assumption. It signified the entire new psychoanalysis and a new concept of the subject:

> For the true formula of atheism is not God is dead—even by basing the origin of the function of the father upon his murder, Freud protects the father—the true formula of atheism is God is unconscious. (Lacan 2004: 59)

The murder of the Father in a symbolic sense represents the beginning of the new era of the subject. Kant in his transcendental idealism methodological put God in the noumenal sphere as a thing-in-itself (*Ding-an-sich*). In essence, in the world of the phenomenon, God is no longer shown by his presence/absence. Located in the non-perpetual area as a matter of autonomy, he does not work in the world. But his regulatory nature is regulated by categories that point to the area of ethical validity (freedom, responsibility, what is valid in the sense of a being that should be but is not ... *Sollen—Sein*). Lacan had to assume, in the original canonical way, the assumption of God's existence. In order to attain the regulatory function of psychoanalysis or its *ethics*, God has been thought necessary from the horizon of the openness of encounter in reality. But in this piece from the *XI Seminar*, Nietzsche's formula for the death of metaphysics, *God is dead*, wrongly takes on the true "credo" of atheism. The position of atheism must be negative. Instead of the ontological markings of the being of God, atheism explicitly denies his existence.

The thesis about God's death definitely does not belong to the thesis of atheism. On the contrary, it is a methodological position of exclusion of the regulatory function of ethics in Kant's terms of value. As Heidegger interpreted, nihilism in the assumption "God is dead" means the abolition of the metaphysical position of the philosophy of subjectivity and a demand for the reallocation of all the previous values. Therefore, Kant's foundation of subjectivity and ethics with the postulate of God denotes the centre of Nietzsche's criticism of the idea of the subject (Heidegger 1961). It must be paradoxical that Lacan, by returning to Kant, only establishes the anthropology of his thought related to the *thing-in-itself*. God is unconscious, which means that the overall effect of consciousness in building a subject is somewhere outside or beyond the Real as such. It did not really appear on the surface of things like a transparent thing. The Real signifies the encounter of the imaginary and symbolic order of things. The subject is aware of this encounter in such a way that he does everything as if he is not aware that it is real from the encounter of dreams, imagination, fantasy and the symbolic order of culture. For a subject with a visual fascination with the body, it might be the decisive focal point.

Als-ob or *as-if* seems to be Kant's true formula for ethics. *As-if* values are valid, though they belong to the regulatory action in the sphere of the practical mind. *As* God exists, or the ontological notion that he is unconscious, the starting point might be Lacan's paradoxical defence of the subject. It seems that the subject has the functions of a subject, but it really does not operate as would be appropriate to the subject. No doubt, it is unconsciously articulated as a language. God as unconscious (What? Who?) from the position of the thing-in-itself or the Real constitutes the entire universe of human experience that is assembled in language. Is this then an (unconscious) theology of the subject with a psychoanalytic dilation of the necessity of its clusters, so that at the end of this dialectical process it comes to the "naked" truth of how the Real is just what the subject poses as his world in the medium of language? The answer from Lacan's point must be confirmed. Yes, psychoanalysis is not faith. But in its unconscious exploration of language as a meeting in real life, it reveals an attempt to reach out to what makes the essence of faith in God. It encompasses an alliance between God and man in a speech that presupposes the Other and the Names (of the Father) that it would attain to be the creation of that real world in the outside world (Lacan 2013). The decentered subject cannot be marked as "a lord in his house". Hence, can we then even talk about the essence of the psychoanalytic creation of the subject as a language of the unconscious creation of the ethical horizon? In other words, the decentered subject is created by the view of the Other and in the Other, is it being re-created to be lost in the Third—to God or to what is structured as unconscious—the language or symbolic order of the world beyond the principle of pleasure?

The phenomenon of a *reality show* in the "theatre of the world" from the point of view of participants or actors is just like this—I do not know how to trace myself. From that, it really rises to phantasmagoria or realistic fiction. What we see is not what we really see, but the object of our gaze. The view constitutes the subject at an imaginary level. However, the view also constitutes an object at the symbolic level. That is why it can be said that, for example, fantasy literature is represented by a rigorous and rational analysis of imagination as a real mirror. Regardless of that, what Lacan is certainly talking about could be the origin of all postmodern assumptions that media is realized as a simulacrum (Baudrillard) or that systems and codes are determined hyper-realistically (McLuhan, Lyotard; Zima 2007: 251–276).

In understanding the position of the subject, Lacan directs the problem to the next viewpoint, which is imaginatively the beginning of a subject's analysis in his psychoanalysis. At the stage of the mirror, we are faced with the narcissistic identification of the self (*moi*), namely with the Other or the Mother represented as the other of myself. I look at the Mother, who makes me look to the outside world. Above the incest taboos or beyond the symbolic order of culture as a prohibition, the Mother replaces the Father by making the symbolic fall as an object of sublimation. This is happening at the stage of the mirror as an imaginary activity that is projected into another and is alienated:

> The ego is an imaginary function. (Lacan 1991: 36)

At this level, identity might not be established in stability because it is mediated by the desire of the Other. In this mediation, it is a natural state. In it, the subject does not exist without the protection of the Other. The imaginary has represented the area of the unconscious in the form of the chaotic state of the natural. It can only be overcome by the individual entering into the articulated language system as a symbolic order of culture. The protection that comes from the Other (Mother) introduces the individual to the symbolic world of the Other. So the language will always be maternal. Speaking of the subject means "giving" unconditional love, and that love stems from giving to another what makes his being self-sacrificing. It gives him an immediate touch, so he can become a person.

Lacan's pairs of oppositions or dualities are imaginary/symbolic responses to the contradictions of nature/culture. The Mother is natural, and the Father represents a system of cultural sublimation. Therefore, it is sublime according to the Father/Law that forbids. In the Old Testament, the Lord cannot be depicted in pictorial form because iconoclasm has been marked as the essence of elevation (Boehm 2007: 54–71). Neither in word nor in image can God be represented. The ban or symbolic function of culture is to overcome that primordial, natural state of a person's need for the Other as a means of self-protection against death. The subject cannot, therefore, arise only from the imaginary, because he lacks the articulated language that unconsciously (nature) translates into language. Unlike Hegelian dialectics of history, which are directed to the natural order of a civil society, which includes the state (reconciliation of concept and reality in terms of the absolute), therefore, in the most realistic and most general of all the determinations, Lacan tries to avoid the necessity of overcoming the logic of the nature of culture. An alternative to the dialectical overcoming/abolition process (*Aufhebung*) should be that the constitution of the subject occurs within the symbolic order of language. Again, we come to language-in-body. The symbolic order of culture is determined by language. Indeed, the horizon of the world will only be open until language is articulated as a meaningful world of signs. Let us see the consequences of that turn in point of view.

The symbolic order is simultaneously defined by a double operation: (1) fear of castration and (2) freedom to overcome castration as a loss of natural connection to the imaginary. However, the very figure of the Father who names and annuls language by banning the incestuous connection between the Mother and the child is obviously a figure of cultural sublimation. The Father's Name is represented by the Law. His symbolic figure necessarily falls. The subject, therefore, has a double function: on the one hand, by going out of the narcissistic phase of the mirror in which the Mother gives the child the natural power of protection from the outside world of chaos; and on the other, by taking over what this relationship allows to overcome duplication. That is what the Father/Law prescribes as a universal ban. Of course, it is about suppressing the destructive power of nature. Because it derives from the imaginary relationship to the world, the order that is already established necessarily leads to the subject being split between natural and cultural. No doubt, in this fracture there is a free space managed by uncanny networks of desires.

The Marquis de Sade in his works radicalizes Lacan's dialectics of desire. For him, the crime cannot be asserted as a symbolic suppression of nature in culture that serves the control of desire, and therefore is historically "castrated", rather than precisely originating in the instinct for life itself. Nature as a chaotic order of the imaginary originally opens in the impetus for life. Hence, sublimated lust should be always active, just like repressive sublimation. It derives from all the historically derived fantasies about sexuality that surpasses the boundaries of culture (Lacan 1966; Ons 2006: 79–89). In that sense, the transgression cannot be, therefore, that only the boundaries of the sex/gender historical link between sexuality and the society of natural customs are crossed. It is at the same time the desire to return to the state of the unspoiled naturalness of order. In this, language removes the fissures of the Father/Law, according to which the symbolic order of history always shows itself in the signs of the history of the fracture, the holes resulting from the uncanny power of primordial desire/lust. In this middle member of the dialectical theory of psychoanalysis, Lacan has opened the problem of overall contemporary culture in general: How can we effectively overcome the gap, fracture, flaw between chaos and order, desire and mind, body and spirit?

The true beginning of psychoanalysis is not, therefore, Freud's theory of sexuality and the unconscious, but Nietzsche's "art physiology" or "vitalistic semiotics", outlined in his original essay *The Birth of Tragedy from the Spirit of Music*. In this book appear the mythological figures of Dionysus and Apollo. Their struggle designates a historically unprecedented horizon of all traumas between nature and culture (Sloterdijk 1986). The problem is that Nietzsche seeks to overcome the overall metaphysics in the separation of above and below, the Being and beings, the spirit and the body. Nietzsche does this from being beyond as the critique of broken and fractured bodies in chains. The return to the original essence of life goes through the subversion of a culturally subordinate body. Criticism of Christendom as an overturned Platonism is the turning point of life without the tyranny of value. The will to power as the eternal return of one and the same historical position might be identical to the work of the scientific history of the circular motion of capital. So the body is not set as Being, but rather the body should be simultaneously an essence of Being. It is the completion of history in the sign of the circular motion of One and the Same in the figure of a superhuman. As we know, this figure resolved the mystery of the end of history.

Superman cannot designate an uncanny biological monster at a higher level than the overwhelming contrast between man and animal, man and machine, nature and culture. Nietzsche thus opened the way for modern psychoanalysis. He deconstructed the devastating power of cultural sublimation. In addition, he pointed to the ideological function of language in religion, philosophy and science.[2] Only art remained the last area of a tragic relationship to the world. However, because it is in its essence unquestionable to the articulated language of the unconscious, art is far away from unconscious and conscious. Moreover, art is a sign of the tragic gap between the imaginary and the symbolic. It does not belong to either one or the other, and life as perpetual being is the true event of its "reality".[3]

The fundamental function of the Father is therefore also twofold. On the one hand, it impersonates a new order or articulates language as a symbol of history in the sign of morality. What is moral is not at all eternal and permanent, but historically justified by the banning of the original power of desire. The Mother belongs to nature and imaginary, and the Father represents culture and symbolism. In an attempt to keep order in balance and not to turn the relationship into structural violence against the original desire as the beginning of unconscious sublimation in language (culture), the Father, on the other hand, as the false, symbolic self, must prevail or to be killed in the last stage of historical transformation of Mother/Father, imaginary/symbolic. The latter is at the same time as the "former", because it is a real field of manifestation of this apologetic scheme which Lacan socializes. As Marx in the system of Hegel's dialectics critically destroyed the whole logic of Absolute history from the second element of the Hegelian system—civil society or the sphere of the economy which lies in the core of the objective spirit—so Lacan, at the centre of his theory of a decentered subject, introduced the figure of the Father/Law as a symbol and a trigger of history.

Language, therefore, should be included in this order of the cultural manifestation of the ideological signifier of history. The horizon of the world opens with language. But at the same time, it closes its apparatus, because in saying the language it has already been "alienated" from the original power of speech. In language, it conceals what originally happens. Originally speaking, the language of the drama of the existential project before it was banned expresses the openness of the world. The tragedy of this position is that language articulates ontological perversion. Instead of the truth of the tragic Being, language speaks metaphorically about *what* is forbidden. So language in a symbolic sense represents the talk of fiction and illusion. We can thus say that Lacan's genesis of a decent range of subject, subordinate and fragmented, but at another stage of symbolic representation, is identical to Marx's understanding of ideology as true of alienated Being. Ideology, therefore, necessarily belongs to the area of language awareness as world consciousness. It can never be a false awareness of the true Being (society, culture, life), rather than just an articulated language of conscious "lies" or, better, categorical flags, delusions, illusions about the truth of Being. That is the meaning of that turn in the critique of the critique of ideology that was so pleasing to Sloterdijk in *Critique of Cynical Reason*:

They know what they are doing. (Sloterdijk 1983: 5)

The Father/Law knows that it must act so by pretending not to know that the truth of the symbolic order of language is always in the suppression or reduction of the primary desire of the imaginary. The Father should, therefore, be aware of the oppressor or an empty signifier of history legitimately determined by the direction. It is empty because it reminds us of Hegel's concept of substance–subject derived from something that goes beyond the function of the subject. So this represents the transcendental ego in the form of an absolute spirit. The Father/Law signified the name of history. It happens by turning off and it dictates and prevails on the imaginary and symbolic in that uncanny state that is more real than reality itself. The shape of capital assumes more reality than reality itself. The form of the spectacle of visual fascination with the body is additionally more realistic than any empirical fascination with bodies in the media representation of the body. For Marx, real-world history is determined by capital as the advancement of science–technology, and overcoming it requires finding a new subject/substance in the unmanageable original production that has the features of artistic work (Sutlić 1987).

This parallelism of Marx and Lacan is, of course, a formal one that is also true of the parallelism between criticism of the political economy and criticism of contemporary culture as a stock of neuroses, frustrations, traumas and pathological forms of psychotic behaviour. But here a correction must be made immediately. This does not mean that the ontological problem of history in Marx's overcoming of Hegel's logic of the absolute spirit is identical to what Lacan psychologizes about on the verge of Hegel, Heidegger and Freud. While in Marx's destructive dialectics of history, it is just about to overcome a third member of capital as the Real and is generally exposed as being involved in the commodity (nature) and money (culture), the imaginary and the symbolic, in Lacan the Real appears in a crypto-analytic relationship. Logic, therefore, cannot be identical to Hegel–Marx's view of overcoming/abolition (*Aufhebung*) oppositions in ascending to the higher level (Žižek 1989).

Lacan speaks in one place about the fracture. This is a gap between the conscious and the unconscious by an individual entering into a symbolic order of language. The subject has been duplicated in the language, so the abyss is hardly noticeable in the language. The symbolic horizon of the world as language is therefore not the linear overcoming of "beautiful souls", in Hegelian terms, from the stage of the narcissistic mirror to the acquiring of the identity through the Father/Law in language as the articulation of the unconscious. This "royal" subject fractured after that into a decentered position between conscious and unconscious. It actually "does not yet know" what it is talking about. We should be able to emphasize that Lacan refers here to the necessary duplicity of the subject in relation to the dreamer who interprets his/her own dreams to others. The fracture necessarily articulates exactly this enigmatic decentered process of the production of the subject (*décentrement du sujet*; Lacan 2004: 164). A contingency, the uncertainty principle and dreams are also reflected in the analysis of the concept of consciousness in Hegel and Nietzsche. Unlike that already mentioned, from structuralist thinking, the problem is completely different. The fracture at the level of the symbolic construction of culture cannot be overcome by denying the unconscious.

The symbolic does not disappear imaginatively. On the contrary, the voice of the imaginary, its inertia, is still heard in that gap. At the very instant, when I think of myself and I like it, I think of and love the Other. The dialectical process of psychoanalysis might be different from Hegelian dialectics in that imaginary stage, albeit the symbolic discourse of the Father in the creation of the subject is not overcoming the Mother in the imaginary creation. The rupture between the two forms the meaning of discourse as a symbolic articulation of language in that necessary glance at the original I which echoes in the "alienation" of the Other. Lacan is at the same time structuralist and deconstructionist (Zima 2007: 266). The subordination of the individual to the rationale of language as the power of sound discourse is the structuralist idea of the governing structure of the subject. But, on the other side, the back, seemingly Derrida (Derrida 1978) refers to the ambivalence of the subject and his discourse, with the difference that he "believes" that it is possible and necessary to make sense of the discourse. But how? Overcoming the rupture or closing it up with something like the third one? By adding to the analysis de Saussure's and Jakobson's language, Lacan deals with the symptoms of unconsciousness in the character field (significant). These are the network of symptoms that make up the meaning. The symptom, one of the key terms of Lacan's psychoanalysis and the whole of later neo-Lacanian theoretical psychoanalysis in the critique of contemporary visual culture, is determined by a new label. By expelling another signifier, he is established in the field of consciousness of the subject (Lacan 2004: 280). In everyday speech, the meaning of such signs according to the subject is unconscious, and they arise from metaphorical and metonymic relationships.

Only this can be said about the *rhetoric of the unconscious*. But it is not a term of unconsciousness, rather it is unconsciously just determined. This rhetoric constitutes it. So the rhetoric that constitutes it unconsciously rests on the pre-ontological assumptions of speaking in the language. In this respect, the term "ruthlessness of the unconscious" is inappropriate. This rhetoric, on the other hand, cannot produce merely the art of speech in transmitting messages to the Other, but an articulated speech codified by the tradition of speaking in the community. Language is taking on here the real condition of the "rhetoric of the unconscious". But language might be constituted in the primary possibilities of speech as thinking of the world and as primordial communication with the world. Looking from the inside, Lacan's unconsciousness does not stem from rhetoric. It is, on the contrary, the openness of the world's horizon in the mode of an unconscious subject.

In the foreword to Anika Lemaire's book about Lacan, he unequivocally says:

> Now I confirm that language is a condition of unconsciousness. (Lemaire 1977: 12)

How should we understand this attitude? As overcoming the symbolic order of the imaginary? As evidence of the "eternal reign" of the Father/Law over the natural or original marking of the subject under the auspices of the narcissistic mirror of the Mother? It is only now that the problem of the relationship between what was in the interpretative sense the main theoretical task of Marx in his early and in his late writings (*Economic-Philosophic Manuscripts of 1844* and *Capital*) can be addressed. This rupture in reading Marx when it comes to the structuralist reading of Louis Althusser has been a fatal mistake not just of interpretation, but of a total misunderstanding of Marx's destructive dialectics (Althusser and Balibar 1971; Sutlić 1987). Structuralists borrowed the notion of epistemology (*coupure epistemologique*) from the phenomenological analysis of Gaston Bachelard. Thus, Althusser separated the abyss of the young Marx period and the texts on alienation in the era of ideology, and the late texts from *Capital* at the time of scientific analysis. The result is not only a matter of turning in the mind, but of consciousness of the gap between the original philosophical result that can be *seen* in structural alienation (*Entfremdung*) of a man being in the very essence of historical events and the unconditional rule of the logic of this alienation in the age of science and technique. The fracture that Lacan speaks about seems to be of the same methodological and epistemological rank as the fracturing or cutting on which Althusser has come to the scene with a scientific interpretation of the continuity/discontinuity of history regarding the self-development of capital and work.

If, for instance, Lacan is now in the self-reflection of his thinking that the Other—language as a symbolic order of culture—determines the first, imaginary horizon of the creation of a subject, then the madness between conscious and unconscious is nothing other than a madness in the essence of language. Language is, namely, unknowingly coming to the stage of self-reflection about itself. The subject signified the emergence of the conscious from the unconscious in the sense of the continuous operation of reflection on the boundaries of the language or the boundaries of the symbolic constitution of the subject. In other words, from the context of Lacan's thinking it can be said: *what* is historically happening with language might be just "the thing" of language that consciousness determines the boundaries of its world. Although the formulation sounds like Wittgenstein's sentence, the meaning is that the symbolic horizon appears in the very language above the superiority of the subject's self-consciousness. Being aware of yourself means to assume that gap between imaginary and symbolic. The language precedes the unconscious. But what is the language as such: thinking or Being? Being in language designates being like *that* which we determine by word to be. However, to say that it is unconscious, or to say, like Lacan, that God is unconscious, means the original event of the Being in his display being attributed to the modern construct of reality. Even more directly, does not the decentered subject in its addictions to the Being in the age of the modern world of the image appear only as a result of the deconstruction of a "strong" subjectivism in favour of a "weak" subjectivism?

Did Lacan, through decentering of the subject, reach the same level as Heidegger's thinking from the very beginning of that fundamental problem? Such an attitude would be against Lacan's own declaration. Being occurs only when *Dasein* in its Being-in-the-world opens the horizon of the event (*Ereignis*) in language. The decentered subject is nothing less than the subject that "at the outset of Western metaphysics in Hegel's absolute spirit system" spoke as a language of essential equivalence of thought and Being. When Lacan unequivocally says that language precedes the unconscious and is unconsciously articulated as a language, then the power and powerlessness of the other (Father/Law) or symbolic order present in the universe are to liberate their own imperfections in the original event of the world. In Marx's words, that language precedes the unconscious means something exceedingly distracting in the understanding of history. The extinction or the possibility of an inalienable existence of man as a capital good precedes the possibilities of his freedom in an unmanageable state. This is the fundamental turn of Hegel's logic, but also Marx's destructive dialectics. The past gains its meaning only from the future. We must pave our intentions in advance, starting generally from that crazy turn of thinking.

The horizon of that truly free event of Being and time lies in the original future, not in the past and present. Thus, the naïve setting is left to Marx and after Heidegger starts from some of the temporally occurring "originalities" of the existential Being, beings and essence of man in the past. The Greek world was a starting point, but not the nostalgic image of reconciliation between the original (*arché*) and the alienated. The primacy of the temporal ecstasies of the future in the idea of communism with Marx and in the thinking of the original event with Heidegger is not at the level of the ephemeral events of the beginning of history, but in an event that goes beyond the entire horizon of history. This is important, because Lacan's psychoanalysis is a problem in the transition between "nature" and "culture" (imaginary and symbolic) of a decent postmetaphysical "narrative" about the world that is in the gap between Marx and Heidegger.

The decentered subject, therefore, cannot be merely the one who, instead of Descartes' *ego cogito*, might now say that it is a subject that should be "conscious" as a result of an unconscious articulation of language. On the contrary, it is the subject that no longer has its centre anywhere else but in the gap between the imaginary and the symbolic world. In an attempt to hear the voice of the imaginary in the symbolic world, the language itself must always be so constructed that it precedes the verbal "cries in the desert" of the ban, power, law. The power of the language preceding the subject of the unconscious is the historically established event of the encounter of the imaginary and the symbolic in the Real. What about a mystery, then? Is it real at all? If Freud's "revolution" in the subject's understanding of Descartes' *cogito ergo sum* was that he showed that the act of the subject's thinking stems from where I do not mean, but I am not thinking of where I am from, then Lacan's psychoanalysis turns to Fichte's formula I = I (ego = ego) in the direction of the sign of equality. The subject is constituted beyond the side of narcissism when there is a contradiction between language and expression (symbolic code and imaginary consciousness). The pre-decessive I as the very language that governs me is still necessarily "alienated" by myself, because in that crack the decentered subject must realize a third one to first speak in the Other as the third. What is it, or, better, what is the third?

Nature represents symbolically or culturally codified nature. Its order of chaos might be arranged to such a degree that in the modern world we can say that nature is no longer nature if it is not bioculturally or culturally transformed nature. Heidegger was referring to this turn in the lecture *The Question Concerning Technology* by analysing his own concept named *enframing* (*Gestell*; Heidegger 2000). The new subject is not a man, but rather science and technology that sets nature as a presence-at-hand one that serves something, a famous image that he submits. The hydroelectric plant changes the natural course of the river. Obviously, this turns the river into an energy source for humans' purpose of exploiting electricity because of their needs. Culture in the sense of the symbolic order of meaning might therefore already be the subject of the operating system. The only difference lies in whether this subject is centered or decentered.

A society that is driven by individual consciousness appears in the unbroken horizon of the relationship between Super-Ego and Ego. Even when Freud, in his triumphal establishment of the Ego, Id and Super-Ego, comes to the social or cultural construction of the problem of sexuality in all its traumatic manifestations, he does nothing more than psychologize Marx's anatomy of civil society as the source of all unconscious frustrations and psychosis (Freud 1982). Whether society might be merely a derivation of a structure or a set of subjects, it has no fundamentals in itself as such. Citizenship or the subject of modern society, therefore, occurred as the result of the scientific-technological creation of needs that govern the human almost as an ancient mystic force. So the economy (of lust) precedes the politics and culture (of lust).

Capital in Marx's notion of history is hence represented in the structural network of mutual social relations. But it could be something even more significant. As we know, capital has represented a *matter* of setting rational regulation of the relationship between human and nature. In that perspective, society does not precede capital, but its other nature in the symbolic exchange of things between humans becomes independent as a new signifier. Thus, Baudrillard's concept of simulacra and simulation (culture) is only a semiotic elaboration of Marx's original scheme. For Marx, social relations in capitalist society are merely meaningful relations between things. The symbolic construction of reality derives from what is the essence of the symbolism. And this is some attributed "value" as a substance. From it, all possible forms of exchange of goods/things are formed. The capitalist ideology governs the social relationships of global capitalism. It is Super-Ego or more realistic than real, and not any old or new political ideology of liberalism.

If we keep this in mind, then Lacan's entire psychoanalysis with the development of the narrative of a decentered subject should be accommodated by what Merleau-Ponty critically figured out of the horizon of the phenomenology of perception. We have seen that Lacan himself has also shown that we are in the "theatre of the world" or *speculum mundi*. We are being watched in the theatre, rather than being those who look at others. Merleau-Ponty articulated the problem of sexuality and psychoanalysis as a problem of something that makes phenomenologically possible communication about sexuality and unconsciousness. What allows communication to a decentered subject has to be a change in the perspective of thinking about the self-constituting view of the person. The Real in the encounter of the imaginary and the symbolic is represented as the unquestionable and unreachable area of realism in which the encounter of imagination and desire forms language beyond the principle of pleasure. The gaze might clearly be not just something related to observation and visualization. The question of whether language is an image or an image of a language is a fundamental ontological question about the essence of the contemporary culture of visual fascination with the body. Why, therefore, can psychoanalysis not be a credible interpretation of the pattern in which the same picture no longer shows or is represented, in which all the signifiers and marks out of the area of the unconscious have lost their "meaning" and no longer speak anything of the phenomenon of emptying the obscenity, eroticism and pornography of visual culture into the white holes of the disappearance of the body itself? Lacan's theory of images will help us move closer to answering the question.

So what is a *gaze* for Lacan? We have already indicated the direction of his thinking about a decentered subject in relation to the phenomenological analysis of gaze (*regard*) at Merleau-Ponty. Obviously, it is not just a matter of world observation. The perception of something comes from the worldly openness of Being and beings. The gaze is an insight into the essence of something. Insight does not just assume visuality; that is, it perceives the subject based on thinking performed by Descartes and Kant, as one who sensitively seeks objects outside their own body, due to their primary ability to know the world as a space–time of the appearance of objects. If Merleau-Ponty's notion of the body has come primarily to the world-accessible object, then the position of the subject in the notion of what is the essence of the phenomenon should also be significant. By looking it comes out of rootedness in my own "house" of the subject, so that what I see at the same time changes my own view. Lacan moves in the direction of understanding the view that from the point of view of the subject—the starting point of psychoanalysis—denotes the inevitable possibility of raising awareness. Every single awareness could always represent the creation of one's own subjectivity.

In other words, the consciousness that is constituted by the gaze of the Other undermines the original power of the subject's perception of the fact that there is a certain fracture or crack in it between the observer and the object of perception. The view is not just "my view" in terms of *my* worldview, but rather has a structure of perceived views. In the analysis of Sartre's point of view in his work *Being and Nothingness*, Lacan confesses to Sartre the view he understood from the dimension of the existence of the Other. But Sartre's existential psychoanalysis has been programmed in its phenomenological perspective, because it does not notice that in terms of the Other I see the gaze as such. Seeing the *gaze* is only possible when I see the gaze of Other who has watched me all the way. At that point, the *look* is constituted as a subject. Lacan's proof of this could be found in the painting of Francisco Goya as catching the look of the Other. The sight of the Other is seen and it is precisely from it that comes, for example, shame. By creating a feeling that changes the perspective of the spectator, the function of the subject has been dramatically changed. He looks to the Other as the function of desire and lust (Lacan 2004: 93).

But what does that desire really want? If the view is in the function of desire, then it is obvious that the view is never just a neutral view of an object. The body that is shown to the world through the eyes of the Other excites the desire for it. The aesthetic glance of the subject also includes some structure of the desire for it. It does not have to be, and never is, a small desire to possess the object. The body is therefore found in the intersubjective network of meanings. Since Lacan's theory of the subject is beyond the reductionism of the thinking subject who sets objects and assumes that the subject itself is set to another, desire is structured like a language of unconsciousness (Braun 2008). Where desire arises is a worldly articulation of the phenomenon. Seeing and observing, therefore, involve more than a mere aesthetic vision and observation of something. Image theory seems essential to the constitution of a decentered subject.[4] It can only be derived from the way in which the subject is placed in this new psychoanalytic notion of the world between the unconscious mode of consciousness and the world. The answer to the question of what this image represents is the answer to the question of the limits of language and the world from the perspective of the decentered subject as a visible and linguistically articulated world. Do the symbolic constructions of the imaginary world in that real one come as a meeting of one another, or does the image always have the surplus of meaning of the Real irreconcilable to the act of *imagination* and symbolization?

> I must, to begin with, insist on the following: in the scopic field, the gaze is outside, I am looked at, that is to say, I am a picture. This is the function that is found at the heart of the institution of the subject in the visible. What determines me, at the most profound level, in the visible, is the gaze that is outside. It is through the gaze that I enter the light and it is from the gaze that I receive its effects. Hence it comes about that the gaze is the instrument through which light is embodied and through which—if you will allow me to use a word, as I often do, in a fragmented form—I am photo-graphed. (Lacan 2004: 106)

I am like an image, as a subject, which means that I am like an assemblage of pictured spaces or a photographed world. But looking at the

Other is constituted almost a priori. Imaginatively in the stage of a narcissistic mirror, it suggests that the image is not present in the imagination. On the contrary, the image is quite illuminated by the meaning of the world as an image. I see, and they see me. This means that thanks to the experience of fractures, it is the departure or abandonment of Kant's classic transcendentalism of consciousness. However, this could not be the surface or the world of phenomena behind which a *thing-in-itself* works, and which is made between two worlds, noumenal and phenomenal; rather, it always continues the only logic of the sublime. Lacan's view is that the existence of this fracture between two worlds allows the viewer to see objects as images because it is purely visual. The body as an image is painted in the other body as a picture, and the look in the function of desire leads to the fact that the structure of the unconscious might be essential for the process itself to perceive the world as an image.

So Lacan defines three fundamental concepts in his theory of image: (1) *image*, (2) *écran* and (3) *tableau*. All these concepts are organized in the same relationship, and in almost absolute terms. The origin of relational aesthetics popular in the age of visual communication with the extended concept of the image must be largely derived from its image theory (Lüthy, in Blümle and Hayden 2005: 265–288). Painting takes special care. The ideology that forms the basis of the imaginary stage of the subject's development belongs to painting, with which humans have a historical relationship of mild contemplation and the sensible pleasure of the gaze. Like Merleau-Ponty in his work *Visible and Invisible* in which he dealt with Cézanne's painting, so Lacan goes on to analyse paintings in the historical era from the Renaissance to Cézanne and Expressionism. Stains and whites painted with a brush on the surface of the "image" open up as the underlying image problem. But it should immediately be said that Lacan does not consider images as creatures, whose hidden meaning should be revealed by the interpretation of artistic creation. Instead of questioning art history and art as a work of art in the medium of painting, here the question is what the painter always creates and what drives him, and what he sees as an artist of that artwork sees as an image. The meanings of the image refer, therefore, to the structure of events outside all the social, political, psychological and psychoanalytic analyses of the artist and his creation. According to Lacan's notion of art, there is obviously some kind of "sublime" relationship. The reason he does not think that psychoanalysis can help us to illuminate the act of creating art is that painting as an event goes beyond all the psychological processes that stand in the background of the creation itself. At that level, Lacan follows the phenomenological analysis of Merleau-Ponty.

The aesthetic feature of what is pictorial is subordinated to the discursive process of painting as its higher meaning with respect to the image viewer. The image represents an expression of a subject that articulates it against the world. What is shown in the picture for Lacan is not even a sense of the aim or purpose of any picture. Touching Cézanne's experience and his apple drawings shows that apples are not what the apple opens, but stains and shapes that point to another kind of relationship. The image signifier, however, cannot transcendentally be granted an instantiation beyond and above the image. Although Lacan takes the example of Cézanne's painting for his argument about the concept of the image and the subject, it is precisely in the *XI Seminar* in which the new theory of the image of a decentered subject is explicitly developed. Cézanne's turn from a geometric perspective to the openness of the world is not analysed from the inside. The view defines the function of the building and is in the field of the visible, while the figure indicates a kind of "stain".

Considering the painting of Holbein and the icon, Lacan comes to an understanding of the equivalence of the embodied and anthropomorphic view (divine and human). The illusion of perspective painting was based on the technical construction of the "behind" view. Therefore, the depth of the view reaches the illusion of the view. Modern painting with Cézanne left that illusion. Instead of the technical construction of the depth of view, it has returned to the world of the appearance of the image itself as the surface. From it "stains" are opened. The look of the picture itself now comes from the front plan. So the emanation of the divine in the image (icons) and the anthropomorphic trace of presence are now lost in the visibility/invisibility of the eyesight itself. If we keep in mind those matters, then we should comprehend the picture exactly from that point of view without a centre, or better without a superior viewing angle with which the entire symbolic order has been established. The question posed by Lacan about where the vision is of a painter in contemporary painting denotes the decisive question of his entire theory of a decentered subject. Indeed, where does the gaze of the "subject" look at the picture as an artistic object? Where does the viewer formally structure the subject? If there was always a look back and forth, as Lacan says in the *XI Seminar*, then the question is where it is now that the image gave the sense or meaning of beauty and sublime beyond the image itself. Where, then, is now what was behind and beyond?

The historical artistic process of the deconstruction of the image of the icon through the representational model of the Renaissance to modern art is largely signified by the disappearance of figurative (referential) painting and the emergence of abstract painting. It is interesting that both Lacan and Heidegger use these terms under so-called quasi-determination. The grounding of the picture, hence, corresponds to the disappearance of depth and the linear perspective. With modern art, the gaze is not directed at some element of the image, but rather on the image as wholeness (Lüdeking, in Boehm 1994: 344–365). I (myself) am the subject of the painting—the painter—set in the view function. Moving the hand on a canvas that is stained with brush paint, as in Cézanne's painting, corresponds to the loss of complete control of the subject. What Lacan points out is that modern painting is what is materialized by stains and lines, but in that act of materialization, there is still something behind and beyond. In the second turn of the same, his attitude might be identical to that of the samurai codex: the sword runs his hand, not the hand the sword. The subject of the painting cannot lie in the sovereign ruler of the image. Its sovereignty, on the contrary, takes place in the midst of something that is not beyond the power of painting, nor behind the view that constitutes the Other and is permeated. No doubt, the step in developing a decentered entity as an unconscious articulation of language is, even more, a reason for strengthening the paradoxical link between phenomenology and psychoanalysis. Lacan is submitting just that to his theory of painting. The subject, in fact, will be physically engaged in the openness of the world as gaze, body and image. But, unlike Merleau-Ponty and Heidegger in the analysis of Cézanne's and Van Gogh's painting, Lacan nevertheless, in the very openness of the phenomenon of the world, sees the primacy of that unconscious.[5]

Lacan does not explicitly signify a subject as the first-person singular—I (*moi*). Self-reflection on one's own psychic processes (feelings, experiences, fantasies, desires, thoughts) represented the beginning of the subject who is founded by its intentions and desire to move in the world as such. But the subject always denotes the unity of formal and real existence in this One expressed by desire or lust. Thus, the subject is always unconsciously a field of manifesting consciousness in the process of self-development from the imaginary, through a symbolic function to "realization" in the encounter of the imaginary and the symbolic. Desire or lust has no fixed point of its own realization. Unlike the need that is the constitution of a subject in a need for an object that can be imaginative or real, desire or lust is represented by the continuous power of the libidinal economy. Under the notion of economics here one should understand the symbolic structure of the unconscious in the "management" of its own limits of desire or lust. There is a need for biological instincts which are either satisfied or not. But desire or lust might be a constituent part of the subject as an unconscious articulation of language. In the line of the imaginary and the symbolic, desire or lust should determine the entire horizon of human existence (Reckwitz 2008: 52–68).

Without a language that is (semiotically) codified and embodied in the subject as a network of relationships, there is no possibility of pictorial representation of the very structure of desire or lust. The semiotic theory of language, which becomes the basis of the theory of new media, should be summarized such that the signifier always refers to a sign and is marked in the circle of another signifier. Moving from one label order to another cannot be a radical cut with the previous order. In Lacan's triad of imaginary–symbolic–real, the subject develops into the meanings of Mother–Father–Son–Daughter. Like McLuhan's media theory always refers to other messages, media to another medium, so the signs of the unconscious in language itself always refer to other signs of the unconscious. This means that it is not same as in Hegel's dialectics of the totality of truth, which could only comprehend the point from the third member of the triad as a synthesis of contradictory elements, but the truth of the subject in its development is shown in every member of the triad. No doubt, it does not appear imaginatively in the symbolic, but rather in the structure of the Real, and additionally, it constantly appears as a desire for the prevailing state of protection in the stage of the narcissistic mirror. The imaginary, however, does not disappear in the light of the symbolic codification of culture. In the "dark night of the unconscious" we are faced with the process of returning to unrestrained conflicts in real life as the inexhaustible and necessary structure of desire for realization in the future.

Lacan's psychoanalytic theories of painting can only be derived from the idea that desire as the primary means of incarnation of a subject is at the same time a desire for what is expressed as a lust for the Other as a desire to give-and-see. This shows how at the level of the appearance of the image and the body there is something there-behind. That "there" carries with it the labels of the previous there (transcendence). The immanence or presence of the image as a body or the body as a picture becomes serious only when the bursting moment of showing the subject to another subject is more than obvious. Giving-to-see means to give one's desire or lust for the look of the Other manifested in the singular gaze that goes beyond the form of seduction. The body, hence, cannot be a subject of seduction and seduced by an object. Don Juan appears in Camus' existentialism as a figure of absurd existence. By neglecting women, it does not matter that they are copied into beings. Don Juan represents the "medium" of the seduction of consciousness. This develops in the dialectical process as a consciousness of the very root of the absurdity of the world. The separation of Being and existence shows the insurmountable basis of the absurd Being (Camus 1991). Basically, Don Juan might be a seducer just because he is self-seduced. The desire for the Other requires the "subject" of the game to realize the imaginary as unconscious. The language of lust in the seduction game manifests itself as historically—symbolically—constructed, as the final foundation of culture: a man seduces a woman in the play of mutual desire to seduce the Other by wanting not to conquer her body/object, but to enjoy all that gives the body a substantial unity.

What Sartre did in his existential psychoanalysis in *Being and Nothingness* led to the unbroken dialectic of "master" and "commodity" (sadism and masochism) conflicts based on Hegel's dialectics, whereby only the ontological perpetuation of the social relation between the "magical universe", which can never be transformed into the transparency of desire, and form of oppression and self-submission, since these forms are eternal and contingent. This was precisely the key place for a critical deconstruction of Lacan in his theory of the subject. The gaze should be constituent of the being subject. It becomes a condition of the visual openness of the unconscious in the image—the body being given to see the Other.

What Lacan specifically wishes to say in his analysis of painting and art we may assume in the way in which he phenomenologically describes the notion of the gaze, which does not relate to any material trace and how the image appears. Looking at a picture by Cézanne, it appears in a non-appearance mode. Mont St Victoire is not represented as a material trace of St Victoire; it is not the only occurrence. The stains and traces of paint on the surface of the image are as real as the mountain is not shown to be "real" or "symbolic". Hence, the mountain cannot stay in the distance, and it should not signify a "symbolic" representation of something sublime, as in icon painting or Holbein's iconographic representation of Christ in the *Crucifixion*. Losing the depth, surface, distance and proximity dimensions reveals that the view of the painter himself is embedded in the image of the world. From it, the picture is shown in its semitone openness as a pure view of the body itself (images). The metaphor in which the tradition of metaphysical history belongs to the imaginary, to which Lacan adds up in his picture theory, can only be regulatory. This metaphor does not replace the symbol or allegory in the "empty transcendence" of the world. Simply, metaphor can only be conditional on how and in what way the body-image as the subject of the painting opens to the Other in an unconscious desire to give-and-see to the Other.

The analysis should be impeccable from the point of view of the psychoanalytic theory of a subject that is unconsciously articulated as language. We should know that the phenomenological analysis of the image is, of course, the starting point right there where new elements are being developed and decomposed to comprehend the overcoming of videocentrism in contemporary culture. But still, a fundamental problem remains. If Lacan left the mimetic and representational model of the image that ruled until Cézanne to turn to the image of the body as he unconsciously placed the subject's structure in the desire to paint the world or in the desire to participate in the theatre of the world, then he obviously accepted the improper assumption of contemporary art that the image is primarily a result of the communication process between the subjects/actors of art in society, culture and life (Paić 2008: 31–80). Given-to-see as a picture-body to the Other means in advance to be in the theatre of the world.

The premise of contemporary art seems just a vulgar temporality. As we know, contemporary art tries to be extended right "now" and "here". If there is no longer anyone behind "now", just those "there" in front of us who are acting in the theatre of the world, then anything goes in the pseudo-events of the time of body-image. Hence, the timelessness of contemporary art is reduced to a constant currency. Communication could be determined to be just like a community of subjects/actors. Being-between means, in addition, to be seen and given-to-see. What Baudrillard calls the *ecstasy of communication* does not refer to the unconscious desire for co-acting in the game to be viewed as the interplay of meaning, but rather what ecstasy means in visual communication. Standing is etymologically the meaning of the word *ekstasis*, the mark for that mode of temporality of the body-image which can be called immersion-in-the-present. So digital images are *immersed* in virtual reality (immersion), in immaterial space–time without a fixed centre. The time of ecstasy of communication represents the present that should be constantly reproduced. In such timelessness "lives" contemporary art from Cézanne onwards. To be a moment and live in a moment means embodying that moment of an instant measure of time. Cézanne considered it just like the unity of picture–body–look. Succeeding in the event of the very life of the image surpasses the distinction between spirit and body, the eye that sees the object that observes me. Being in between, in the gap between the subject of painting and the "essence" of the image, means ultimately being at the ecstatic moment of *image*, *screen* and *tableau* as an interaction. Keeping this in mind, we can conclude that communication in the digital landscape is a sign of the necessary exchange of information, which means the physical presence not only of real persons but also their twins in the form of avatars and fictitious persons. There is nothing strange in that along the way, and nothing uncanny, simply because how the subject and object matter in the era of digital communication might be about the way in which the process of creating actors is generally developing.

The communication model of the image, therefore, is not the one which holds that the image has been signified as a "mirror" of the social, cultural and living conditions of existence. That is to be said decisively. Society, culture and life are not even objects of the avant-garde and neo-avant-garde art of the twentieth century, but rather the iconoclastic revolution of art that wants to construct a "new world" from the idea of the world as a real event in which imaginary and symbolic, the life of society and culture, are very closely tied. We could not forget that the condition of viewing opportunities as the unconscious wishes of the subject to be given-seen as a picture-body to the Other stems from already established communication in the theatre of the world. That is why all visual arts are now necessarily becoming performing arts. The body as an image appears in its mode of existence as a given-to-see to the Other only when the communication model of the image might be realized in the living theatre of the world. That *speculum defeated* which Lacan mentions, but does not develop radically, can no longer be a mimetic and representational model of the theatre of the world, because the image that the former theatre of the world inevitably assumed was lost, abandoned, disappeared from the stage or the spectacle of the world. The new image must be communicative and derived from the idea that the theatre of the world happens in life itself, which means in real time and in the virtual space. The origins of such images are the events of the theatre of the world in the entire creation of the most radical artist of the theatre and pictures in modern art—Antonin Artaud (Chiesa, in Žižek 2006: 336–364). Let us see how he performs his unique project of art transgression at the very core of his singular life.

3.3   Artaud and the Theatre of Cruelty

Artaud's *theatre of cruelty* has its "image" in the "painting" of Van Gogh's painting. This is a picture of the mimetic and representational history of art. It can no longer present something "real" and cannot "represent" something irrelevant and overwhelming. The image that comes from the world being itself a theatre sets itself into a lively body-to-stage. Artaud's theatre of cruelty opens the way to the body-image as a visual fascination. But the work that is happening in life itself is not an avant-garde construction of society as the life of art in what we call life itself. The problem which Artaud posed by his action—the event of image and life as a body in the theatre of the world—emerges from the framework of the psychoanalytic theory of the subject. However, from Derrida's deconstructive philosophy of difference, we might say that this seems very paradoxical. Artaud's theatre of cruelty deconstructs both in the way that it goes beyond the question of the subject as an unconscious articulation of language and subject matter as a decentered network of the meaning of differences. Neither sexuality nor Christianity (an urgent structure of desire and symbolic order of control of lust for sublimation in culture) is even in the neo-gnostic synthesis of the direction of Artaud's theatre of cruelty. But even less could such a "project" be understood by starting from the communicative function of the body–image–speech. Precisely because Lacan and Derrida are concerned about the relationship between corporeality, visibility and speech to the thinking of the decentered subject (of differences), let us try to find out from Artaud's art the direction beyond psychoanalysis and deconstruction.

Already in the text devoted to Van Gogh's painting, we come across a radical criticism of the image representation model. Although in this text, apparently, the concept of Catholic sin is opposed to "erotic crime", that is to say symbolic bargaining as opposed to the imaginary chaos of liberty, to Artaud only the body of the murdered man "suicided by society" of the perverted depravity of social institutions is an image preceded by any contradiction between "crime" and "punishment". To Artaud, Van Gogh and his madness have an ontological sense of justification for art as the only true world (Artaud 2003: 255–262). Being beyond social boundaries means being in the very centre of life. In Van Gogh, Artaud recognized, of course, an unquenchable duality. Unfortunately, this is not considered a psychiatric case. Van Gogh/Artaud's madness is just a picture of a civil society fearing the transgression of its symbolic order of "normality". Art does not want to change society here anyway, as was the programme of the historical avant-garde of the first half of the twentieth century and the neo-avant-garde of the 1960s. That is, Artaud's theatre of cruelty is radically different from the matrix of seemingly identical demands for overcoming the limits of art and life. And just because the social revolution is a profound decline in art in everyday life, Artaud's direction is the greatest possible requirement that art can have of itself in an authentic way after we are faced with Van Gogh in painting. So art does not change the imagination of the symbolic order of the world, it is uncannily and horrifyingly *real*. That uncanny and terrifying thing lies in art itself. Let us recall the verses of Rilke in that context from the "First Elegy" of *Duino Elegies*:

> For beauty is nothing but the beginning of terror, which we can just barely endure, and we stand in awe of it as it coolly disdains to destroy us. Every angel is terrifying. (Rilke 2014: 5)

Artaud claims that in Van Gogh's painting, "there is no wavering, no vision, no hallucination" (Artaud 2003: 279). If there are no such things, what else is there still alive? Without an unrealistic, unobtrusive future, without the psychoanalytic obsession with the inner world of dreams as a traumatic unconscious, it seems that for Artaud, Van Gogh is represented as a paradigmatic artist for the pure concept of art by any means. It is not disclosing a *new one* to the world, but rather the evolution of the eternal novelty of the cycle of birth and death of life itself. The body in which the image of such art is happening is life without any internal and external perceptions, without the clash of impulses with the religious bans of "erotic crime", without the external conflict of social institutions of art with the grammar of imagination. Van Gogh's painting is the immanent transcendence of life in the life of the body itself, which is not just the human–superhuman. It should be the body of nature and spirit, substance and subject, space and time of the encounter of the human with the event of the simultaneous uncanny and horrifying flash of the world here and there—in the centre of the image where the fire burns on Earth and the madness derives only from the fundamental perversion of society and its symbolic cultural institutions. Artaud unmistakably says that Van Gogh's painting is nothing but the idea of painting itself:

> Most of the world, Van Gogh was concerned with his pictorial idea, a fanatical, apocalyptic, terrible visionary idea. If the world needs to be

arranged according to its own matrix, it is necessary to transform its rapid rhythm against the mental life, the rhythm of the occult celebration and the city square, before returning it to overheating in the melting pot. This means that in the payoffs of the old battered Van Gogh at this hour of the apocalypse, perfect apocalypse, and that the earth should be able to tear it off with both his head and his legs. No one ever wrote or painted, sculpted, modelled, built, invented, for anything other than actually just to get out of hell. (Artaud 2003: 275)

Going out of the "hell of the Real" could be possible if he comes down to the "hell of the imaginary" or if life is carried into the "purge of the symbolic". The former represents Van Gogh/Artaud's alternative to the social revolutions of the nerves themselves. The latter belongs to the aesthetic design of the world as a technology of life itself. This completes the idea of a historical avant-garde in the performative-conceptual theatre of the world. In it, every event might be necessarily artistic action. However, this might only be the case with the transformation of the object into an artistic subject. We have already mentioned that in this way Paul Klee introduced a turn to modern painting. When objects are obscured, then the very view of what is "postponed" returns as a "postural" view of the so-called subject. Therefore, not so self-confident yet distorted, the "image" of social relationships between things that make up the essence of spectacular representation in global capitalism does not affect the essence of those "things".

Society as a network of communicative relationships between remote entities/actors, however, is represented as the only space–time of such closed art in which the body constantly strikes at its own spectacular borders. But only society may be a spectacular representation of the idea of capital, as Debord showed (Debord 1994). The closure of the signifier and the signified is completed in the sign without any message to the Other. In this "symbolic exchange of objects" (Baudrillard), society transforms itself from the position of subjectivity into its Janus face—the objectivity of things. A consumer or hyper-consumer society is merely the ultimate form of representation of the spectacular disappearance of the difference between sociability and cultural capital. The picture of that turn would be exactly just what is represented in the image of the digital age: the omnipresence of the media in the universality of the uncanny gaze. The transparent society of the global age is no longer the subject of the visualization of the world. It is quite the contrary, the object of spending its own empathy, which makes sense in the perverted situation of the world as such.

This is extremely important for two further reasons.

First, modern art has opened the new world only from its own bounty. The freedom to paint objects outside the iconographic ban on the appearance of Christ's body differently than it was written in the canonical texts of the Christian tradition had to be a positive iconoclasm. The disappearance of human figures in modern painting and their replacement with an abstract figure is the same as the disappearance of the divine from the world. Therefore, modern art endeavours to find out more about the aesthetics of the work by trying to open a new world of image events. Avant-garde art radicalizes iconoclasm in its negative form of absurdity. The body as an image is the life-long self-determination of art-in-motion. That movement becomes the living as such. It is therefore inevitable that the movement of life is directed at the movement in what drives the real power of life. Society is the modern home to the subject, or, better, as Heidegger says, only society has represented the result of modern subjectivity (Heidegger, in Jaeger and Lüthe 1983: 18). The art that changes society itself in the direction of the new social power necessarily invokes any version of its "social revolution". The contemporary image in the media representation is thus always a disadvantageous social or communicative product between the subjects/actors of visual communication.

Secondly, what Artaud does in Van Gogh's painting is not a direct way to the centre of "the dark night of the unconscious", but to the centre of the "bright night of the apocalypse". From its body-image comes the disappearance in the clear light of the moment. It is a radically different path and an alternative to social revolution in art. That is why Artaud goes beyond all the avant-garde programmes and the limits of Surrealism as the artistic movement of the imagination's imagination. To illuminate the Earth: this is what Van Gogh wanted from the fire of the Earth itself. It is the image of the world of the *new one*. The body is burning because it should be the earthly source of light. The "rhythm of the occult celebration" according to which "the world is to be repaired" takes on the life-art of the world. But this might be not a mimetic model of the world's representation, nor a representative model of its representation. That was what led Lacan to the *XI Seminar*, when he begins with the theory of images from a phenomenological analysis of the gaze. But even more radical in the reading of Artaud's theatre of cruelty was an interpretation of the method of deconstruction of metaphysics by Jacques Derrida (Derrida 1978).

For Artaud, the theatre of cruelty is primarily "affirming the terrible and, moreover, unimaginable necessity". Derrida asserts that this does not mean destruction, but rather a confirmation of a new manifestation of negativity. It certainly implies only that such a theatre has not existed. Therefore, its image does not come from the source of the chaos in terms of the scandal of tragedy's origins in Greece. We can argue that it is emerging from the future that brings new birth to itself. So in all the elements of life where the theatre of cruelty has been manifested, it has to confirm it. The body in "blood and flesh", in spirituality and the sublime, to which I am a living witness as an artistic event of the artist's work—that is exactly the direction of Artaud's projection, which really was a fascinating event in the art of the twentieth century. Bringing the state of immortality to death as far as it is imaginable as living, restrained through the social institutions of art—that is the goal to be pursued. If, as Derrida says, what is called *cruelty* is still a mystery to us, it is only because the theatre has been the place of the separation of spirit and body, real and imaginary, Being and the beings.

The mimetic image namely determines the metaphysical fort of such separation. It shows something beyond the incarnation of the truth of the Being itself:

> The theatre of cruelty is not a representation. It is life itself, in the extent to which life is unrepresentable. Life is the nonrepresentable origin of representation. (Derrida 1978: 234)

Cruelty, according to Artaud, is therefore another name for life. The humanistic boundary of the classical theatre is that life has always been presented and represented by human life. Since the human is only a reflection of such a life, it is obvious that Artaud cannot imagine that an individual subject might be a figure/actor. Therefore, Derrida is right when he says that Artaud wants to end the mimetic concept of art and Aristotelian aesthetics that lies at the very heart of Western metaphysics. Art, therefore, cannot be an "imitation of life," but life is "imitating the transcendental principle that brings us art to re-communication" (Derrida 1978: 234).

Let us stop here. Derrida suggests that Artaud's concept of the theatre of cruelty follows the overcoming of not only the concept of the mimetic image throughout the history of metaphysics (religion, philosophy, politics), but also of representationalism. It is a decisive thing that only the theatre of cruelty should be the original force. But it still needs to become the privileged power of opening that place (*topos*) from which the imitation of life is destroyed. This is not at all controversial. Artaud thinks of the living theatre as the body-images of life's life itself. However, the most realistic of the Real, the monstrous and the scary, is that the power of negativity of one's life is not gained in "this" life "here", as in so-called real life, but rather only in the artistic self-determination of life. Life is always born again in a new time beyond the metaphysical timeframe, which to Aristotle rests on that "eternal now" (*nunc stans*). Can such a picture of the new body of the theatre of the world be anything but different from the one that follows from the model of life communication?

The vicious circle of the deconstruction of metaphysics is exactly what Derrida is trying to deconstruct. Life as an imitation of the *transcendental principle by which art leads to re-communication*? Is this not the main problem with Artaud's interpretation of Derrida's metaphysical horizon and the psychoanalytic theory of the decentered Lacanian subject? Re-communicating in the theatre of cruelty is guaranteed from above. Obviously, the transcendental principle allows this "innovative communication". For Derrida, this transcendental principle that is broken up into the *différance* of Being and beings marked the emphasized notion. Directly from itself, it only gives rise to thinking of differences. For Lacan, this means the same monstrous and scary real power. It only allows it to be unconsciously structured like a language. By moving this principle from above to "below", which makes Nietzsche discover the body's blindness without the latter principles, and puts Van Gogh at the ground of a fire burning in the image "without wavering, vision, hallucination", only realizes the long-standing history of metaphysics. Nothing else and nothing more. Now, however, it shows that Artaud, in his turn towards theatre, has never existed; he thinks of the theatre of the world in the same way as the disappearance of the body as an image. Paradoxically, he abandoned the representational model of painting and theatre to formulate the body against the iconographic task of the text throughout history. How is that at all possible and what designates the ultimate reach of the project known as the theatre of cruelty?

We have already said: cruelty might be nothing else than a synonym for the brutality and ecstasy of life. The first step in establishing the affirmation of life as a negation of the semblance of the imitation of life and its presentation to the picture/theatre of classical metaphysics is negative. God leaves the stage and disappears from it. But this is not the affirmation of atheism in the theatre, nor the secular form of the claim that God is dead. Any negation in the process of chatting in the world at the same time is an affirmation of the new. However, this is not about "the new God", but rather about something beyond the theological assumption that God exists as a supreme being. Undoubtedly, Artaud sounds just like a radical atheistic artist of life. He seeks to deepen the primaeval divine against the perversity of the institutional God of monotheistic religions. However, God in that manner represents just another name for the symbolic order of the perversion of Being in the ideological discourse of the Lord who managed and governed the world. Although Artaud's thinking was a modern supplement to Nietzsche's fundamentals and ideas, the origin of that thinking belongs to Heidegger's assumption about the *oblivion of Being*. The ontological difference denotes the differentiation of Being and the essence of Being. When the other being, the essence of Being, is attributed to a being that replaces being so as to assume the attribute of the highest Being, ontological "perversion" has been at its root. The "lower" being as the very essence (God) is completely overcoming the field of openness of the Being, and thus darkens it throughout the history of metaphysics (Heidegger 1977, 2000).

Artaud has considered a stage or scene of theatre plays as a drama with the theological discourse of the Lord (of history). Throughout the history of the theatre, the voice and the will of the *logos* are mastered. And that is the will that underestimates the actual event of the theatre in something

that even precedes the *logos*. The structure of such mimetically representational theatre is metaphysical. On one side is absent God as the creator/
drama of the drama, and on the other performers who speak the text. The
content of thinking in the text of the speech is assigned to the roles of
actors, so it is already the discourse of logocentric power. In this interpretation Artaud is the main point of Derrida. Almost every single text
derived from the metaphysical tradition carries that logocentric trace of
enrolled power. Artaud's theatre of cruelty is the attempt to turn around
such a metaphysical tradition of separating God as a creator/director and
the player/figure as a text interpreter. Speech articulated in language, and
language spoken in the text written in the theatre, must be radically
deconstructed (Derrida 1978). Instead of imitating the creative power of
God (director/author), who stands in the absence of the representation of
the text "published" by the act, which is only interpreted but not questioned, the theatre of cruelty might be the confirmation of life itself.
Turning to the primordial power of life leads through the liberated bodies
beyond that of speech, language and text. Such a theatre is determined by
a pure visualization of the body itself as an image. It fascinates participants of the event. Instead of the voyeurism of representation, instead of
the narcissism of the modern obsession with the subject as the origin of
my own self, the theatre of cruelty requires its rootedness in the visual
ubiquity of the world. New signs of one-off life replace the repeatability
of permanently written speech.

The stage (scene) subordinated to the rule of speech as a language in
the articulated text must necessarily be representatively organized.
Speech in the metaphysical environment is always talk of the separation
between the Being and the beings, God and human, and other beings.
In the phonocentric system as a prerequisite for moving to a linear series
of abstract (Arabic) letters, Western metaphysics is, in fact, from the very
beginning constructing a real symbolic power of language (Derrida
1978: 236–250; Lacan 2004: 48–74). Derrida and Lacan, deconstruction and psychoanalysis, approach the analysis of language on the same
imaginative ground, but with different solutions, because of the suspicion that it is precisely in that puzzle of the entire history of our play of
existence in the theatre of the world. Artaud, by the very means of
expression and insight into the essence of the metaphysical "perversion"

of life, can be considered to be the one who most seriously understood the instruction of Nietzsche: that the life of the very body on the stage of cruelty has assumed upon itself the supreme task of surmounting all the "true" Being. Art beyond the semblance of the truth and the truth of the illusion occurs through the singularity of the artist's existence as number (communication), image (visuality) and word (body). We are faced with a new triad of the postmetaphysical framework of any imaginable new "culture" (Paić 2007: 13–30).

In this regard, Artaud in his Nietzschean way of thinking prolongs the ecstasy of life in the situation of the most radical turn ever possible in the theatre. Why are we talking about the turn of the theatre, but not the overcoming of the representational model of the picture and the theatre? It might be obvious that the notion of the image as a representation of social relations is also preserved in the concept of the society of the spectacle. The theatre, as well as painting all the way to the end of the great era of representation, was based on "dramatology" as the "iconology" of how the drama plays with speech (Fischer-Lichte 2004). Therefore, the body has always been in its theatrical history with the screen, the projection surface and the small mirror image of the rule of the absent presence of the power of speech. When speaking as a logocentric dungeon of language exercises its task, the body sacrifices its freedom of insubordination of the image related to the event of the very body in favour of the sublime and the beauty of the transcendental principle. Only this principle allows speech to "have" its signifier, a signified and a sign (Artaud 1988). Nothing else drives things forward.

But since Artaud claims that it is not to be forgotten, it is rather the *perversion* of the theatre itself in the midst of Western history that is the decisive step that links the thinking of Nietzsche and Heidegger. The perversion of theatre might be essentially the result when the iconoclastic structure of the image itself becomes *self-explanatory* in the face of the original burst of lifestyle. Hence, the origin of the oriental mysteries with the cult of Dionysus, as has brilliantly been described by Nietzsche, and Artaud adds up to it, is only a flash of that primordial towards which the theatre of cruelty does not turn around to return to something vanished. In memory of this event, which has been preserved in the underground feasts of bodies without the sublime and beautiful gestures of the classical theatre of representation, the parallel history of that "forbidden" in the history of the play has passed away. The carnival and the theatricalization of the image at the time of its postmodern inevitability since the end of the 1960s are nothing but an attempt at the original freedom of the body itself in the events of the transversal/queer that the festival returns to the centre of the visual culture of the contemporary age. Certainly, Artaud did not even see any liberation or celebration of sexuality in the act of sex as such. Moreover, his rationality in declaring Christian Catholicism after returning from Mexico pointed to a completely different vision of what the body still has to strive for in art. This could still not be the gnostic way through the body as "dark matter" until the total disappearance of the body in the pure light of the energy of the visualization of spirituality in the "other world" (Chiesa, in Žižek 2006: 336–364). The problem is evident in the definition implied by such a self-explanatory expression of the body in the theatre of cruelty.

Under the statutory representation of the image as text (speech and language in the articulated system of writing), the theatre "uses" the body just as a function or network of functions. From classical theatre to a modern civic drama, the body is not seen differently than the textually overlaid stage of the stage. The scene is determined by the incarnation of the word. So the words speak, and the body should be quite silent. Therefore, the visibility of the body is only possible to represent when it comes out, speaking in Lacan's parables, to have nothing or just something unreadable, almost indecisive. What is "there" behind it is no longer God or the universal Lord of speech in the theatre of representation, but rather the communicative omnipotence of the body in permanent motion. Instead of the idea of a theatre close to the idea of God as a ruler in terms of creativity and authority, Artaud's *The Crucified* should be based on a "self-representation of pure visibility and even pure sensitivity" (Derrida 1978: 238).

Let us keep looking at the essence of Artaud's image/body-image as a visual fascination separating the matrix of the avant-garde transformation of the idea of life and art. If the return or turnaround to the primordial comes only from the future, because the theatre of cruelty has never existed, then Artaud's project becomes radical postmetaphysically in the image instead of the rule of the logos as text. It can even be claimed that the project is an *iconic turn* or *visual turn* in the 1990s. Artaud's idea of theatre as a life-giving image of the body-image in the spectacle of the life force itself was a decisive turning point with the representational model of the image. Specifically, such a theatre, in its turn towards the body-image of pure visuality and sensitivity, must destruct/deconstruct speech as language and speech as text. This means to return, or better said to go in the direction of a future return, to poetic literature, the unity of dance, music, performative and conceptual art that has evolved from the end of the 1960s to the underlying forms of contemporary art. However, the poetry in this total turn of life as art has to become theatrical, and the theatre of poetry must take on the dimension of indecision and the endowment of words at the limits of what is expressible and physically reachable. But what it is important to point out is that the notion of cruelty to life or life itself has nothing in common with the literal explosion of "communicative" testimonies of sadism, horror, bloodshed, sexual provocation and body crushing on the stage of a contemporary theatre. An experiment with that transgressiveness (overcoming) in the contemporary theatre obviously should go through all the ecstasy of the body like pain. The liberation of the body from speaking as God in the discourse of the Law/Father represents a terrible and painful experience of traumatic events of one's own and the body of the Other.

Artaud, therefore, in the theatre of cruelty has only radicalized the programme of the historical avant-garde that art should become life's power to overcome social reality. By radicalizing the idea of the "revolution of art" from the "revolution of life itself", he could not continue in the direction of Hegel–Marx's dialectics to overcome (*tollere, conservare, elevare*) the notion of the idea of theatrical theatre with the idea of the total body theatre (*Gesamtkunstwerk*). This would be "rational" from the point of view of the logic of historical overcoming of the emergence and being of "truths" and the "semblance" of life without the constructive illusion of reality itself. Artaud's turn is around the pure visibility and sensitivity of the theatre and against the dialectical methods of overcoming/abolition in previous models of the painting and the theatre. In Derrida's style of interpretation to be understood in accordance with Heidegger's interpretation of Hölderlin for the possibility of thinking of the event (*Ereignis*) at the point of Being and time, but with the difference that Artaud has the status of a privileged artist-thinker of Nietzschean inspiration for the purpose of the deconstruction of metaphysics, there is still something disturbing.

Obviously, Derrida has significantly pointed out the direction in which Artaud opens possibilities of the non-representational theatre of the world in the poetic sublimation of body-image (Derrida 1978: 242–250). So the return to body-image is at the same time a turning, not an over-turning (*revolution*), of the overall metaphysical tradition of the theatre at the stage of the world of text. Now the turning point toward the body-image has to come from being the one that the text has always allowed to be a fundamental marker of history. Sensitivity (*sensibilité*) is not opposed to the visual fascination with the body. It is the vivid immediacy of bodily experiences in the world. That is why *plasticity* is *visual* and the visual is necessarily related to the kind of writing that does not follow the logo-centric history of the West. Egyptian hieroglyphs and Chinese ideograms are a videocentric/eccentric writing of differences. The scripture as a tran-scribed speech in the image, immersed in the body of life itself, has the same status as dreams. Such is a letter from the Egyptian field. In the stream of dreams, the visual–plastic materializes speech. Artaud was in contact with Freud's psychoanalysis, but also, in criticizing its absolutiza-tion of the unconscious, he came to the key setting of his postmetaphysi-cal theatre of cruelty.

The body-image performance takes place at a one-off time (singular-ity). This is the time of ambiguity, whose scripture is not written as a text but as a sign of the existence of life itself. A body without a text is not a body without a world. The world of an immersed lifetime in the event surpasses the conscious–unconscious articulation of language as a sym-bolic order of written dreams. The theatre of the world is therefore not the psychoanalytic development of the subject's event as an unconscious articulation of language, but rather the world's only theatre as a con-sciousness of the singularity of the body-image. Instead of a theatre immersed in dreams, the theatre of cruelty is based on hieratical masks of the divine, which precedes God as the Father/Law and the classification of culture as a ban.

Artaud's rejection of psychoanalysis was ultimately the case without compromise. After eleven years of forced residency in a psychiatric clinic in Rodez, where Lacan once visited him and in his diagnosis wrote that he was obsessed with the fact that he would not be able to write anything for years (Artaud 2003: 93–254; Chiesa, in Žižek 2006: 336–364),[6] Artaud radically interrupted any possibility that his theatre of cruelty would introduce the term unconscious. After all, from the very beginning, it is unconsciously and knowingly just a way of bursting the life (cruelty) of life itself into an event of artistic activity in the world. The reason why Artaud radically protests against Lacan and therefore is relentless to him is because Lacan represents the paradigm of psychoanalysis as the "perverse" primary life drama, Freud's fundamental assumption that dreams are in the function of unconscious fulfilment of wishes. The lifestyle in its ecstatic state of reality and dreams, imagination and the symbolic order of marking is not conscious of the unconscious and the desires that submerge dreams. On the contrary, dreams are life's self-confirmation of the power of the body-image in a writing originating from beyond, so as to consciousness, rational language can never be any function of anything else. Dreams are a manifestation of the primordial connection of bodily nature immersed in the picture that the plastic shadow of the war prints of the drama of the unified world as a theatre without God (Lord of Discourse) and as a theatre without the reign of the universal transcendental principle (the ubiquity of the beyond).

Criticism of psychoanalysis (Freud–Lacan) is here, therefore, a radical atheistic version of the symbolic and real death of God. But, as we have already said, that is what makes Derrida's interpretation of Artaud binding: there is no utterance about the atheistic theatre of the world or about the dialectical overcoming/abolition (*Aufhebung*) of metaphysics. Artaud in his turn towards the body-image wants from the future to be-in-the-scene by purifying the divine place. The God of the classical theatre (=metaphysics) is dead. But the death of the established Son of God is symbolic. This projection of the human power of naming the prohibition of primary life in favour of the symbolic perversion of the meaning of life in the rule of the "censorship" of social institutions, and in which Artaud carelessly counts the psychiatric institutions which psychoanalysis justifies, should be the true condition of radical ontological perversion.

What does that mean? Simply, Artaud, the artist-thinker, realized that socializing the text as the power of discourse or the language of history is a condition of ontological perversion: God determines the highest being and thus is the Lord of all things. The problem is that Lacan performed a symbolic construction of reality by providing the possibility of perversion in the imaginary stage of the "original" wishes of the subject for eternal Motherhood as such. But Artaud hated psychoanalysis, because it desacralizes the world and takes away the roaring power of the puzzles of a game of pleasure in all forms of self-determination of life itself. The ontological "perversion" is that the Being, the essence of man and beings were understood metaphysically, but always from perverted life as Being. From the very beginning, life as Being is characterized by an original course of representatives and games (of cruelty) in the name of the Father/Law. What does that mean in its turn? Whether Artaud or Lacan really meant the same, was that fatal misunderstanding the result of an inability to comprehend that the decentered subject in the unconscious articulation of language was precisely his path from the theatre to the "pleasure of visual-sense communication"?

It must not be thought, however, that the paradox is complete, the companionway of thinking of Artaud and Lacan. One was outside the social institutions of power, and the other institutionalized psychoanalysis on Freud's foundations as a method, a "new science" and a "philosophy" of contemporary culture. Here it is not even of special importance that Artaud considered sexual relations through the dematerialization of the original love of the divine. As the disappearance of the classical theatre of representation means the return of the body-image to its dignity of a visually sensitive presence on the world stage, so the theatre of cruelty is the only way of life's drama being the disappearance of the body-image in the purity of the spiritual Being. Astral body-light is illuminated life with self-respect. The shadows of the rascal masks of being in the theatre of the world alone can reach the aura of the divine, which is not a metaphysical God of legitimate tradition. In the end, did not Lacan, in his primary sense, perceive God as an indisputable place of expression of the world as a transcendental source of unconsciousness? The language of Artaud is the dramatic speech of the Nietzschean "prophet", and the language of Lacan is psychoanalytic talk of grounding and precaution, speaking of the subject's boundaries in an "abandoned and empty house".

We have seen that Lacan, in his analysis of Cézanne's painting, came to the same assumption as Artaud in his analysis of Van Gogh's painting. Here the question is not who is right, Artaud or Lacan, or Derrida, with the deconstruction of the image as a mimic-representational model of metaphysics in history. On the contrary, the problem is that the psychoanalytic theory of the subject as an unconscious articulation of language cannot open the possibility of understanding the openness of the actual event of the contemporary body-image. Behind and within this framework, it can no longer be said that the "empty transcendence" of the body-image or its "empty immanence" when there is nothing left behind and when it is all visual and plastic, "there" to the openness of the theatre of the world, works as a *speculum mundi*. It remains, however, throughout this analytic walk on the edge of the body and it is something disturbing. Derrida's interpretation of Artaud's theatre of cruelty as a deconstructing scalpel that crunches into the painful point of all contemporary culture, which moves to the unconscious production of language (the psychoanalytic theory of the decentered subject), concludes Artaud's analysis of the discovery of the *world as play* (Derrida 1978: 250).

The fatal border of the theatre of cruelty is that the idea of theatre as a body-image does not have its limits in the world as a play, rather than in the representation itself. Indeed, the question about the subject of the play might always be the question of *who* is playing *what*. Without authors and actors, without the world, there is no body-image that "communicates" with others in the "theatre" as a *speculum mundi*. Life as a game goes beyond any possible subject–object of the game. In the end, Artaud has set his own "concept" of the theatre of cruelty on the trajectory of Nietzsche in that way that it is exercised by a close analysis of Van Gogh's essay to come to the key assumption that emerges from the frame of what Lacan named the riddle of the overall life of reality—the Real. If the game of life should be performed as an artistic event-action in the world, then no theatre or representation of itself in the theatre of the world can any longer be the play of a subject. This is the fundamental difference between Artaud's concept of body-image and the psychoanalytic theory of the unconscious subject of the view that constitutes the horizon of meaning. In the text *Van Gogh—The Man Suicided by Society*, we can find something that is scary and uncanny about the only thing that matters:

No, in Van Gogh's pictures there is no wit, there is no play, no subject, and no object I would say, because the motive itself, what is it? Perhaps like a leitmotif of topics disappointed with your subject. It is a bit of naked and pure nature, seen as it is when we know it is enough to get it. The witness is that landscape of molten gold, of bronze baked in ancient Egypt, where the huge sun was leaning against the roofs that, as if decomposed, were worn out by light. And I do not know any apocalyptic, hieroglyphic, phantom or shrill images that would cause me to feel that dull feel of the occult, unusual hermetical corpse, with an open skull that would reveal its secret to the stump. (Artaud 2003: 280–281)

The picture "worn out by light" is life itself as a game beyond the brutality or ecstasy of life itself. The time of the moment without utterance, drama, subject is not tragic. The tragic derives from the very incarnation of the image, which is already immersed in "dead light". It seems truly more tragic, even to the extent of the modern loss of the value of illusion. Can we see the way out of this vicious trap by which we have been spellbound since primordial times (*arché*)?

3.4 The Second Death of Culture or the End of Psychoanalysis

There are different interpretations of Lacan's theory of image. All of them start from the fact that its theory of a decentered subject is the key to understanding our contemporary visual culture. At the same time, the deconstruction of the notion of culture is not taken as something that is stored twice in itself:

1. the ideological discourse of the culture itself as the symbolic order of marking; and
2. the disappearance of the discernment of that imaginary in the very notion of culture before the complete dispersion of the symbolic order in decentralized cultural frameworks as a lifestyle and subcultural circuits of action.

From Lacan's theory to a decentered subject—namely, one path leading to the critique of ideology with Marx and Althusser's concept of the hegemony of capital and the state (Žižek); and the other articulating with the poststructuralist theory of an artist subject as the effect of media and discourse in subversive work on changing the social conditions of visual communication (a series of contemporary theorists of visual studies; Žižek 2006b; Mirzoeff 2002). For the former, it will be crucial that the interpretation could be called the re-politicization of culture, and for the latter the re-aestheticization of politics. In both cases, Lacan might be the origin of radical political/cultural resistance to the real order of global neoliberal capitalism. Psychoanalysis as a way of researching an individual subject through becoming the unconscious becomes a theoretical platform of social "revolution". But since Freud–Lacan's psychoanalysis is linked to the critique of ideology and the social "revolution", nothing has happened that is "revolutionary". Already Sartre in *Critique of Dialectical Reason* in 1960 made this encounter with Marx and existentialism in the inescapable encounter of the social revolution of capitalism and the selfish individual *cogito* as a subject of existence (Sartre 1960; Lévy 2005).

However, this encounter was grounded in the wrong assemblage of assumptions. But that was not because Sartre's philosophy of existence and psychoanalysis did not put the subject of an action in the network of social relations at the centre of the matter. It was incorrect because he started from Kierkegaard's analysis of consciousness, and in the twentieth century from the cult of the reception of Hegel, and so Marx, in contemporary French philosophy. It is, of course, mediated by the lectures which were given by Alexandre Kojève and published in the book *Introduction to the Reading of Hegel* (Kojève 1980). The attempt to give Hegel a "human face" in the sense of receiving primacy against essence, a man against an absolute spirit system, was just a step in the direction of individualizing the existential organization of culture against the alleged danger of the new totality. Hegel and Marx thought they were dialectical, constructively–destructively, and not separated from the standpoint of absolute subjectivity. Thus, it turned out that Sartre's neo-Marxist existentialism is the same narrative as existentialist humanism, because now man is perceived as subjectivity with the social (social-class) horizon of his emergence in the world.

Contrary to the binary opposition individual–society at the level of Marx's anthropological materialistic critique of Hegel, that man encompasses the totality of social relations proved to be ineffective for Lacan's theoretical psychoanalysis too. Opposites of the individual versus society, nature versus culture, man versus technology have disappeared from the horizons of human sciences by setting Roland Barthes on "the death of the author" and Foucault on "the end of man". Semiology or semiotics as the theory of the media representation of culture could become a universal method and epistemology of post-science only because it excluded the dualism of man and the surrounding world. McLuhan and Flusser have developed semiotic settings about media or the telematic information society. But the notion of society is no longer autonomously determined apart from technological communication. It is visual (number) that necessarily all that is visualized (picture) and ends with the disappearance of the body (words) in pure information.

Lacan, in his seminars, carefully remarks that psychoanalysis could be a worldview or philosophy, but also neglects the social, classical, historical conditions that determine the development of the psychological dimensions of human existence. In the end, the great discovery of the mysterious concept of the Real, which in no way *exaggerates* that "real" or "reality" (*dinglich* and *wirklich*), defined it as a meeting of the imaginary and the symbolic. History takes its place as a sign of the cultural or ideological history of the rule of the discourse of the Father/Law. As a social form of commodity/goods exchange between people, capitalism presupposes the formal and real existence of capital in science and technology. That is the reason why it is justified to ask the question: Why does every critique of ideology necessarily have to deal with criticism of the social form of capital and the cultural form of its representation and sublimation? Is Lacan's theoretical psychoanalysis a credible critique of the contemporary ideology/culture of videocentrism or the society/culture of the spectacle in which the body appears as the object of the other body, and the subject already has a network of relations between all beings in advance?

Why must it even be so important to warn that the omission of a radical deconstruction of culture today means only the renewal or *revival* of the already politicized processes of culture as a repoliticizing of art (Groys 2003)? First of all, this is important because theoretical psychoanalysis is the basis for the critique of the ideology of a concept of culture as the foundation of the neoliberal globalization of the world. How can Lacan's psychoanalysis be criticized by the visual representation of the ideological discourse of neoliberalism, if Lacan himself already at the beginning of the theory of painting claimed that the picture should be primarily understood from the phenomenological point of view? Is this not paradoxical and uncanny? During the theory of painting, Lacan was reluctant to base the concept of the subject in its strange position of subordination and disagreement. The subject in a decentered condition simply works in a decentralized world. Why would it have been previously labelled subordinated and scattered, in the addictive connections of the Other? The world in a decentralized condition has to emerge as an image of the very subject that, with the view of the Other, constitutes its own "world".

From the beginning of Freud's psychoanalysis, the criticisms of his theory were, as we have already shown, identical to the critical objections to Sartre's existentialism. Namely, it is dispensed from the view that the individual subject is engaged in advance in the network of social relations, class conflicts and ideological-political disputes, and that the individual as such is collectively defined by social practices. Lacan's response to these critiques was in principle identical to Freud's. Psychoanalysis is the theory of the subject. It starts with the individual. But he does not understand it in the modern sense like Descartes and Kant as the absolute creator of the world's knowledge and experience.

That decentered subject is someone who has already been thrown into social situations. But self-reflection in the imaginary–symbolic order faces the Real (the world), so it has the potential for real-world change. Of course, this is not in the absolute sense of Fichte's understanding of the freedom and spontaneity of what I do, which Sartre in his existentialist stage has radicalized with the idea of synthesis *en-soi* and *pour-soi*. His possibilities are to change the real world limited by self-consciousness from the unconscious articulated as a language to the consciousness of actual (world) disintegration in its decentered process. Lacan, unlike Sartre and his "radical conversion" of the second phase of thinking with the acceptance of the Marxist concept (social), opened only the chance for the possibility of change in the most complex concept of his theoretical psychoanalysis. The Real is nothing in advance. It could be said that the categories of modality prevail in itself (possible, real, necessary). In the Real is primacy of temporal ecstasy of future just like openness of an event from which it is possible to socialize and even radically politicize its fundamental ideas. Slavoj Žižek also made this almost paradigmatic in *The Sublime Object of Ideology*.

Let us go over the core issue of this debate. Why is there a revival of the theory of the subject once the question of the object and objectivity after Hegel and Marx has been overcome as a metaphysical problem? A phenomenological approach to the image through the perception of the view was not guided by the idea of the reconstruction of the subject. It is therefore paradoxical and uncanny that Lacan accepted the phenomenological analysis of images and views. We need not forget that it is only conditionally possible to say this correctly. His acceptance of Merleau-Ponty's thinking in the analysis of Cézanne's painting was nevertheless conditional, or, better, methodological, for some completely different purpose. Indeed, the unconscious in the desire or the desire to give-and-see the view of the Other in the picture becomes a decisive shift from the phenomenology of the picture. In order for a subject in his decentered condition to have some reliable starting point, some new foundation in his own bounty, he must reconstitute it in the visual world of objects of desire. The imaginary desire to give-and-see to the Other and see the Other in the theatre of the world should be already symbolically constituted by the view of the Other. It is as if we were to spin in a circle that reminds us of the hermeneutic circle, but in fact it cannot be just like that; rather, it has the inevitable end of thinking in relation to the power of desire.

This view (*regard*) is actually the whole of Lacan's psychoanalytic theory of a decentered subject. But unlike Sartre and Merleau-Ponty, the view is represented as the symbolic horizon of the unconscious production of desires and lust. The view is, therefore, a condition of the possibilities of realizing the possibility of extinction regarding the ideological structure of the language which symbolically governs the view. Therefore, language as a discursive and ideological power of telling the subject, unconsciously elevated to the Father/Law, regulates social relations as objective social-class and ideological-political relations. It could be now apparent that the visuality of the modern era is not the "innocent" visibility of new media as new information-communication technologies. In this seeming "innocence" of the real framework of relationship and structure, the problem of the ideological construction of the reality of the contemporary world is definitely hidden. We always see the curved, from different angles, by parallax and periscope, but never in this respect to the world; there is nothing initially ontological and unchallenged in history as a symbolic rule of language that only allows us to see what we see, just in this and that way. A good example of this might be the film *Parallax View*, in which paranoia is transformed into the only correct theory of political conspiracy as an explanation of what seems real, but in fact is not.

Where has Lacan taken the view? Does the view of the Other, which constitutes the subject of the whole of his historical, cultural and ideological network of meaning, really look into the essence of the world? The answer is not explicitly in the *ethics of psychoanalysis*, but rather in the analysis of the viewpoint as the ontological-ethical position of the subject, which looks at the Other at the same time as the Other, and so comes to the dialectical relation of pervading and changing. The subject of Lacan's concept is structurally determined by his development through three stages: (1) imaginary, (2) symbolic, and (3) Real.

The gap between the symbolic and the Real, as we have seen, differentiates the concept of the subject from Hegelian dialectics. Neglecting the unconscious articulation of language is not a function of overcoming, but is about what cannot be retrieved by the conceptual constitution in its entirety. If Lacan's notion of the subject is unambiguously defined in terms of the dialectical motion of the notion of "lower" to the "more" stage of his own self-consciousness, then the decentered subject is neither empirical nor objective, neither biological nor philosophical, neither political nor sociological-historical, neither constructivist nor metaphysical—but *linguistic*, "*logically*, or based on the logic of the signifiers" (Braun 2008: 19–20). It is, therefore, important to point out that a subject is not something like a self, nor a thing or something determined, nor a being or a substance, though underlying to every possible ambiguity and experience of the world. From the tradition of the metaphysics of subjectivity, Lacan's concept of the subject is not an identity, but "something" that can be understood from the viewpoint of difference and distinction (Braun 2008: 20–21).

The structuralist idea that the subject does not refer to something "real" as such or to other "subjects" other than the sign system that determine what is understood as the Other is decisive for the thinking of the decentering of the world at large. This negativity, a clear definition of the sign system, leads to the subject being considered as a mirror game. Lacan explicitly says, "The game is a subject" (*Le Jeu, c'est le sujet*, Lacan 2001: 164).

Against the philosophical tradition that *hypokeimenon* and *subjectum* understand from a different view, the notion of the essence of the Being of beings and the world at large, Lacan's concept of the subject should be understood in principle as a deviation from the metaphysical tradition. This means that the subject simultaneously appears as the thought of the *logos* and is logically (linguistically) based. That is the main difficulty of understanding a decentered subject. Such an entity at play with language in all aspects of life conceals and breaks down its shrewdness and freedom in language as the horizon of meaning. But if the subject is maintained even after Hegel–Marx's view of the subject–matter dichotomy is overcome, despite all the innovativeness of Lacan and structuralism, semiotics and poststructuralism, the new scheme of the sign, the signifier and the signified or imaginary–symbolic–Real is only a different way of naming consciousness to its stage of "realization" in self-consciousness. In other words, Lacan puts his "faith" in language as the source of all the images of the image, set forth on the basis of the new theory of the subject.

With the view of the Other who constitutes the subject, the condition of which I constitute myself is essentially changed. However, this "Big Other" is not a transcendental (eternal) signifier like God. He is playing with the language and the language game is an empty signifier. It is only in this uncanny fracture between the imaginary and symbolic order of the world that the place of the subject is acquired. It is unconsciously "awakened" only by becoming "consciously" that language itself in its historical being that is logically structured as an indescribable field of reality.

The gaze, therefore, changes the observer and is perceived at the same time. The subject becomes a language game as a game of world meaning to which the view is not subordinated. The image is not an accidental language as a substance. In the addictive addictions of image and speech as language/text, the world in its horizons makes sense. Lacan tried to save the subject from "extinction", giving him a new way of founding an unconscious in the fracture of language itself. But in what way, in the end, is there the impossibility of establishing a legitimate possibility of a complete interpretation of the decentralized world of contemporaneity in the strict philosophical sense of a decentered subject without a logical/linguistic basis? If the subject does not refer to the "thing" that he thinks and feels, and he/she is already in a game of signification, then the very concept of the subject has already been deconstructed as such. The subject is not a "thing", but its homogeneity between the imaginary and symbolic order of meaning appears in a game with the linguistically articulated real event as inexhaustible. The language precedes the unconscious (lust, phantasms, picture).

Lacan's thought metaphysically "weakens" essentialism. The subject is not the one who places "things" on the real horizon of the world. It is a self-contained "thing" of language in its own abandoned house. Empty and desaturated, the subject is unconsciously structuring language in the game with itself and the world. The problem of theoretical psychoanalysis is that the decentered subject in the decentralized world is still a "subject" in the "world". And that means that it is derived from the structure of consciousness, which has to assume that *it* is whence arises consciousness as pure revocation and that Being has the power of annulment and the subject itself. That is where it derives, the subject is the transcendental horizon of the world as "things" in the structural field of meaning. Subjecting in the world begins with a look no longer behind, but "there"—in immanence. Therefore, this immutability of life or Being, in its own time, could be psychoanalytically postponed in the body-image.

Alain Badiou tried to link philosophy and psychoanalysis—Plato and Lacan—in such a way that the ontological problem of mathematics was growing. The idea that ontology assumes primacy over real mathematics is based on the number (one), while in psychoanalysis it is always a fracture between two—the subject and its signifier (Badiou 2008: 201–202). The subject is constituted by the view of the Other. Two in one signifies the splitting of identity that is decentered in its disagreement, so that any further possibility of sharing remains excluded. Doubt is therefore always the duality of the Being and the being, the gender/subject, as the origin of psychoanalysis. But the problem of the ontological beginnings of the idea (Plato) and the duality of the subject in its identity (Lacan) cannot be solved mathematically. Mathematics represents merely a logical–visual view of the language game with the indisputable–indescribable. Thinking from the perspective of calculation and planning definitely leads to the sphere of construction of virtual worlds, whatever else may be perceived by something which means *arché* along the way of metaphysics.

When psychoanalysis, as in Lacan's case, promotes the solving of onto-logical problems by bringing them into the problem of the identity of the subject in his imaginary–symbolic–real world of worldly relations, then its problem is that its future represents what as with Plato always was related to the ecstasy of past times. The memory (*anamnesis*) at the begin-ning returns the narrative to a posthuman language of a method that is neither science nor philosophy, but is somehow related to the determina-tion of what modern science and philosophy are constantly persecuting: the stains/shadows of the past. The subject in the psychoanalytic journey through the station on the path of consciousness is the unconscious artic-ulation of language. Who really remembers what precedes the return to the beginning of the constitution of consciousness? Is it an entity that speaks to the shadow of its own shadows of the past, or is it the language that tells about the history of its "own" history? Time becomes a funda-mental problem in understanding how the subject is constituted by the subject. Remembering, indeed, has an unconscious function. In Jung's concept of the archetype of the collective unconscious symbolic structure of the world, it is always the craze/frenzy in memories that the suppres-sion seeks to overcome, because it leads to traumatic events throughout history. To understand, then, the way of articulation of language which precedes the unconscious, as Lacan pointed out, means to comprehend the historical constitution of language in its temporality.

Lacan's programme of psychoanalysis returned to the subject as a turn-ing point of everything that the subject meant in modern philosophy and science. If language is a condition of the "speech" of the unconscious, then it is obvious that the language of psychoanalysis is the lifestyle of life rather than the true life of the language of life itself. Criticism of psycho-analysis in Artaud's theatre of cruelty can, therefore, be considered as a way of overcoming its boundaries. What are the boundaries of its borders other than the metaphysical horizon of language? For Lacan, language might not be the ontological question of a subject, but it could be an ontological subject in a matter of language. It does not ask what language it speaks in its saying and who speaks (subject?). The language wondered how and where this language, which is a condition of the subject as unconscious, spoke in the symbolic order of culture.

The basic proposition of Lacan is the "denaturalization of nature"; that is, the fact that it is initially meaningless of the nature of the language itself and becomes unnatural (Johnston, in Žižek 2006: 34–55). Unlike Heidegger, whose language's specific use of thinking shows the horizon of the world's worldliness in the event of Being and time, because the language speaks and the subject cannot but construct one's own transcendence of unconscious consciousness and there is a linguistics, Lacan's language might be determined as a structurally understood system of signifier, signified and sign. So language for Lacan represented a network of signs. That must be decisive. Why? Because the pronunciation of the language enables its creation. The consciousness that is constitutive of the subject's position in the new era is enabled by the pronouncement. Between the words of the language and the unconscious articulated as a language lies a fundamental ontological difference. Pronunciation of language and language as a condition of the construction of the unconscious subject are two contradictory concepts of the world. The former is phenomenological and hermeneutic and the latter might be psychoanalytic. For the first, language has to be found in the world; and for the second, the world becomes the construction of the language (subject).

Hence, all that we call social constructivism becomes a new beginning of "nature" as it is always culturally transformed "nature". The subject in its linguistic constitution with the view of the Other precedes the substance. Lacan's "soft" essentialism, therefore, might be comprehended in such a manner that the question of the subject is not performed anywhere outside the cracks in the subject itself. It is the subject of its substance that it must acquire in the act of radical separation from Mother Nature (imaginary) in order to meet new realities in symbolic re-creation. Awe of the eternal Woman (Nature, Mother, imaginary) indeed represents a paradoxical way of negating the contemporary body-image culture as a female body in the function of perpetuation. Men, like in pornographic digital visualization films, are reduced to sex organs: multiplied penises are thrown into holes and empty spaces. The body represents, therefore, the symbolic construction of a world without nature, a totally cultured world without its substance, but fascinating because the subject, at last, ends up expressing its body as language, speech and things among other things.

The visual culture of the contemporary world is represented by the real manifestation of the inability of the body-image to open a new world until it destroys the thinking of the subject from which the objectification of the world derives from the symbolic horizon of postmetaphysical language. So the terms of psychoanalysis are not to overthrow the philosophical tradition as metaphysics, but the postmetaphysical language that can no longer be understood in the original body of life itself. Artaud recalled his theatre of cruelty as the danger of the "weakness" of psychoanalysis with its apology for the unconscious becoming a new power or assuming the function of the new religion of denial in the interpretation of the world as a theatre suppressed/free of desire. Moving from "conscious" to "unconscious", from the spirit to the body, was an inevitable act of deconstructing the history of the culture of the West. But as Lacan's real remainder of the mystery of all relationships between humans, the enigma of social relations that, in Marx's analysis of capital, with its convex shape the perverted form of the world is the alienated world of its being, so the new theory of the subject can only be understood as the new theory of culture regarding the pure body of the visualization of the world.

Culture and society are the results of modern subjectivity. It is a source of discomfort in its sublime form of rationalization of desire, but perverted life itself is in its pure nihilism of value. By theoretical psychoanalysis, the world of visual representation of contemporary global capitalism can only be described as trimmed. And because of Hegel and Marx's constructive–destructive dialectics in relation to the clean surface of things, their freedom to play has been manifested by the inherent contradictions. In any case, psychoanalysis cannot understand the phenomenon and the notion of the image, as Merleau-Ponty and Artaud demonstrated, nor can art retrieve its indomitable path towards the sublime. Psychoanalysis should be simply a method by which society and culture are constantly being renewed in their unconscious-minded power games. With Lacan as the peak of psychoanalysis, he comes to the end of its essential possibilities. In accordance with his famous assumption of the two deaths (symbolic and real) of an object, contemporary visual "culture" represents only the second death of culture. To put it another way, a long-lived subject lives both symbolically and really. Of course, at the death of the subject, it thinks of unity with substance in the realization of the concept and the idea of absoluteness at Hegel and work with Marx. Anyway, culture becomes possible as a value speech only when the subject and the substance are separated.

Thinking of language as a symbolic order of culture obviously cannot be enough. This defines the subjectivism of things and the objectivism of thought. Symbols related to other signs, body-images and other visual phenomena in the world are empty of the circle of power of a subject that enjoys its powerless game, because the game is predetermined by the language rules of the subject itself. The enchanted circle of the dialectics of lust and semiotics of the unconscious, hence, decompose to the debris of the moment when, as Baudrillard has shown in the analysis of Cronenberg's film *Crash*, the body without organs sets it as a purely aesthetic object beyond the *eros*, but also beyond the *thánatos* too.

The visualization of the body is no longer a living or an inanimate body. Therefore, it is indeed a question of how to interpret this turn of the disappearance of culture with its kingdom of subject/language, which goes beyond the question of consciousness and the unconscious, subject and object, the end of society and culture in the pure substitution of life itself, its biogenetic reproduction.[7] Psychoanalysis is just a starting point. It is a concept of life. It was done just like anthropology by Freud and radicalized on other grounds by Lacan. The concept, however, is taken from Nietzsche's "vitalistic semiotics". The life of living matter is represented by the ecstasy of corporeality in all forms of its power (*vita activa*). In the "centre" there is no new subject in the state of unconscious production of wishes expressed in the symbolic order of language. In the "centre" of life now stands a figure coming from the future. That is a superhuman arrival. With its arrival, the opposition of the spirit and the body, the intellect and the lust of heavenly and earthly, Apollo and Dionysus has overcome generally.

The fundamental problem of scheduling psychoanalysis is precisely in what Artaud as an artist of life saw in Van Gogh's painting—an

apocalyptic event of life without fiction, drama, motifs, without unconscious structuring of desire. The image of the visual structure of culture
is the complete evolution of language through its conception of the
means/purpose of communication. Society and culture are now understood by the communication process of circling signs around an empty
centre. Society and culture no longer have a substantive basis. The resil-
ience of the ultimate disappearance of the nullity of physical communication between objects creates the very concept of the subject.

Paradoxically, Lacan's psychoanalysis has long been discarded in the
psychiatric treatment of psychosis and all other severe mental illnesses. In
the neo-Marxist criticism of global capitalism, it conquered due to Žižek
the dedicated status of the interpretation of the critique of ideology. This
is not the outcome at all in Lacan's theory of the subject, but in the appli-
cability of his analysis of the culture of the contemporary world as a
symbolic order of the meaning of the perverted world, or, in other words,
as a visually fascinating ideology. Instead of language, the image has taken
on its "hands" the structuring of the "new language" as the unconscious.
Films, the societies of the spectacle, visual communications, *speculum
mundi*, the predominance of the symbolic of the imaginary in the ideologically created real core, could be the reason for its sustainability, and
when the real culture as the Father/Law language no longer exists in its
imaginary worlds of projection of the future.

The second death of culture is happening precisely in the biopolitical
production of life itself as a body-image without organs.[8] The distortion
of body and image derives from the biopolitical production of life itself.
Such a life surpasses all past values: the right to chastity and human dignity. Life as a biopolitical body-image production surpasses nature and
culture in all their historical contradictions. In this way, culture is a value
and rests on the assumptions of the humanist idea of the subject, even
when it is a decentered place for the empty signifier, in a house that is
empty and abandoned. Lacan's psychoanalytic theory of the subject starts
from denaturalization from a natural standpoint. The subject is exclusion
and deployment (eccentricity and decentralization) from the uncanny
chaos of nature, that imaginary in the symbolic order of culture. Only
this is the reason why Lacan can talk about the *ethics of psychoanalysis* in
dialogue with Kant's concept of moral law (Lacan 1986).

What is, however, crucially determined by the subject if not the cultural order of signs through which the subject can only articulate as conscious of its own historical unconscious place in the world? The order of the signifier, signified and sign in what makes the symbolic horizon of the subject world is determined by the subject's becoming. The time dimension of the future derives from the possibility of changing the causal-teleological model of its "destiny". As Heidegger destroyed the metaphysical self-perpetuation of the causal–teleological model of history, Lacan also questioned the same model in understanding the unconscious articulation of a subject's language. Symbols in the sign of meaning mean the "being" of the subject within a historically determined order of action. But signs do not mean anything by themselves. Only in relation to other signs do they gain meaning. The structuralist theory of the text assumes a relationship between the indented signs. So the subject might be therefore always in relation to other subjects in some structural order. Thanks to that, culture can only be called in that way and nothing more. It is not a superior horizon of meaning in which the subject lies in the world. Conversely, the cultural order has represented the symbolic horizon of the text, and it ideologically seeks to perpetuate the immutable and "fateful" of the writing. To have a radical change in such a system does not break the ontological structure of the symbolic order. It is reconstituted again in accordance with the ruling signifier (social relations that are not fatal but are overdefined only in a historically established relationship).

3.5   Conclusion

When culture itself is "distracted" in its symbolic horizon of meaning, when the world is a horizon of meaning in which the subject is disturbed, it should be necessary to *deconstruct the subject* (Braun 2008: 326). If we comprehend what this is all about, then the turn from the existential suicidal situation of the subject, of which Lacan speaks, and the focus on the opportunities that lead to the absolute freedom of the subject's negativity has been performed. The subject is distraught by suicide in the whole world. In the structural relationship between the subject and the world, the cultural order is symbolically disassociated in that in the very language in which culture is expressed as communication (number), visuality (image) and text (word) reaches the final symbolic restitution of the subject in the world. Its position should be de-subjected, or, better, it has become an intersubjective network of relationships by turning its body towards openness and at the same time closing its apparent freedom to change the world's condition.

The second death of culture in its visual construction of the world in that way might be nothing else than the second death of the subject in the real event of the biopolitical production of life as a pure body without organs. Is such an artificially reproductive life overwhelmed by the traditional oppositions of spirit and body that precisely transform the body without organs and organs without a body, which is precisely substituted, autopoietic, technological? In the former case, the theoretical analysis of Gilles Deleuze and Felix Guattari represented a poststructuralist insight into the reign of a subject without substance, and in the latter, particularly in the criticism of Slavoj Žižek, Deleuze's anti-philosophical method of reigning designates a substance without a subject. Constant oversight of these two decisive words of philosophy from Descartes and Kant to Lacan and poststructuralism is to determine the "destiny" of the contemporary world that still holds the old words of life for new phenomena, simply because the language of the new phenomena has already lost the primordial power of speech in advance. In the society/culture of visual communication and language itself as the means/purpose of communication, the medium becomes a posture of discourse. To imagine a body without organs and organs without a body obviously needs an adequate language of the experimental transgression of philosophy. If we confirm that it matters, then such thinking surely needs something pretty much "more". What if the language is no longer in the world, but rather it could be imprisoned in a closed body, just like a picture without a world?

Notes

1. "The mode of my presence in the world is the subject in so far as by reducing itself solely to this certainty of being a subject, it becomes active annihilation. In fact, the process of the philosophical meditation throws the subject towards the transforming historical action, and, around this point,

orders the configured modes of active self-consciousness through its meta-morphoses in history" (Lacan 2004: 81).

2. "But nihilism is not just Nietzsche's shedding, devaluation, and destruc-tion, but the fundamental organization of the historical movement. (…) For Nietzsche, Christianity is also nihilistic as Bolshevism, and also as mere socialism" (Heidegger 1985: 30–31).

3. "Art as a will to power is the highest form of the will to power. / The phi-losophy? Spiritual will to power! But the latter as the fundamental essence of Being, the essence of reality, is in itself this Being, which itself wants to be one. This is how Nietzsche tries to 'think to the power' of the original unity of the old basic principle of Being and beings. The essence of Being set up should be to be self. The origin of the thought of 'eternal recur-rence' is thus set" (Heidegger 1985: 271).

4. In the context of new media art and theoretical orientations within a wide range of interdisciplinary cultural sciences with an emphasis on the visual or pictorial turn as well as the *iconic turn*, the question of the image and its symbolic meaning inevitably addresses the issues of unconscious boundaries in the articulation of visibility. The decentered subject assumes discursive practices of new media as their space–time of virtual reality. If Lacan unconsciously articulated a language, then the *language of the new media* in full right can be called a digital code that surpasses the opposi-tions consciously and unconsciously in generating new media reality. That language is precisely the decentered subject of a decentralized network of meanings which nowhere has a fixed centre. It assumes the same assump-tions as a *global network society* without its visible centre, whereby all deci-sions and all directions of the actions of the subjects/actors of globalization arise (Manovich 2001; Castells 2000).

5. "'The age of world picture' for Heidegger is a modern age that makes everything a matter of own imagination and preparation. (…) Cézanne's pictures do not serve the overwhelming and completely different. Here, on the contrary, the observable image experience is of crucial importance. (…) Physically engaged viewer position, the bodily presence in the world is exactly what Merleau-Ponty saw as exemplified in Cézanne's paintings. The painter experiences himself as a body among the bodies, he still lives in the 'flesh of the world' and is visible in his paintings. Alberti's eye, on the contrary, as the starting point of the picture is an unconscious eye. It cannot be considered as a body, but only as an optical instrument. It has the same function as the lens of a photographic appliance. Merleau-Ponty

is a turn from a perspective-oriented image of the Renaissance and against a mechanically produced picture of a photograph. (...) Heidegger is seen ontologically by the world, and Merleau-Ponty is phenomenologically, but both are, in principle, close to the image of the world" (Lüdeking, in Boehm 1994: 354, 355, 356).

6. Artaud labeled Lacan with the expression "erotomane": "Compared to lucid Van Gogh, psychiatry is only the last refuge for gorillas who are obsessed and persecuted for the temporary mitigation of the most terrible conditions of human affection and suffocation, have only a ridiculous terminology, a product worthy of their damaged brains. Namely, there is no psychiatrist who would not be a notorious erotomane. I know one who rebelled, a few years ago, at the very thought of lapping this whole piece of this group of the lowest and most unpopular high figures and unscrupulous powers to which he belonged. I, Mr. Artaud said, I am not an erotomane, and I invite you to show me the only element on which you base your accusation. It's enough to show you, Doctor L., just one single element, and you see that clinical symptom on the loss. You are some kind of an ugly bastard" (Artaud 2003: 257).

7. In biogenetics, reproductive life is no longer understood by the act of natural divinity and multiplicity of Being, but rather as a recombination of genetic potential in their complexity. This shows that the question of body-image can no longer be understood by any other than the media. What is the difficulty in a notion such as a body-image as a medium derives from the essence of media? It is no longer a matter of substance or form, real and unreal, alive or non-alive. The media are structured as the alienated language of the entire "culture". From Lacan's psychoanalytic scheme to the subject's advancement, it is evident that the symbolic "real" field of manifestation of a subject in the fear of castration assumes the Father/Law language and abandons the imaginary field of manifestation of that phantasmatic field. The subject is the symbolic construction of the real world. That is the reason why Lacan's psychoanalysis and Marx's critique of Hegel's dialectics are essential points to the other members of the triad (symbolic of Lacan, and Marx's critique of civil society determined by the rule of the economic laws of capitalist production). Both are ideological constructions in order to function as a "natural" course of the "legality" of history. But the problem is that what is real in the constitution of the world of technology has been shown as a symbolic self-realization. For this reason, Lacan's theory of the subject in the modern

times of visualization of the world is inoperable because its ontological quasi-Hegelian triad can no longer think of a turn towards the body without organs that is neither conscious nor unconscious, but language is for such a body more symbolic and not the structured unconscious production of wishes, but rather already pre-constituted by the media, which should be interactive and communicative (Kamper and Wolf 1981, 1982).

8. "Never has the human body—above all the female body—been so massively manipulated as today and, so to speak, imagined from top to bottom by the techniques of advertising and commodity production: The opacity of sexual differences Dim Stockings has been belied by the transsexual body; the incommunicable foreignness of the singular *physis* has been abolished by its mediatization as spectacle; the mortality of the organic body has been put into question by its traffic with the body without organs of commodities; the intimacy of erotic life has been refuted by pornography. And yet the process of technologization, instead of materially investing the body, was aimed at the construction of a separate sphere that had practically no point of contact with it: What was technologized was not the body, but its image. (…) Advertising and pornography, which escort the commodity to the grave like hired mourners, are the unknowing midwives of this new body of humanity" (Agamben 2007: 48–49).

References

Agamben, Giorgio. 2007. *The Coming Community*. Translated from Italian by Michael Hardt. Minneapolis and London: University of Minnesota Press.

Althusser, Luis, and Etienne Balibar. 1971. *Lire le Capital*. Paris: F. Maspero.

Artaud, Antonin. 1988. *Selected Writings*. Translated from French by Helen Weaver. Berkeley, CA: University of California Press.

———. 2003. Van Gogh—The Man Suicided by Society. In *Tarahumara and Other Works*, translated from French to Croatian by Marija Bašić, 255–262. Zagreb: Litteris.

Badiou, Alain. 2008. Rimbaud's Method: Interruption. In *Conditions*, translated from French by Steve Corcoran, 68–90. London and New York: Continuum.

Boehm, Gottfried. 2007. Ikonoklasmus: Auslöschung—Aufhebung—Negation. In *Wie Bilder Sinn Erzeugen: Die Macht des Zeigens*, 54–71. Berlin: Berlin University Press.

Braun, Christoph. 2008. *Die Stellung des Subject: Lacans Psychoanalyse*. 2nd ed. Berlin: Parodos Verlag.

Camus, Albert. 1991. *The Myth of Sisyphus and Other Essays*. Translated from French by Justin O'Brien. New York: Vintage.

Castells, Manuel. 2000. *The Rise of the Network Society: Economy, Society and Culture: The Information Age: Economy, Society and Culture*. Vol. 1. 2nd ed. Oxford: Wiley-Blackwell.

Chiesa, Lorenzo. 2006. Lacan with Artaud: j'ouís-sens, jouis-sens, jouis-sans. In *LACAN: The Silent Partners*, ed. Slavoj Žižek, 336–364. London and New York: Verso.

Debord, Guy. 1994. *The Society of the Spectacle*. Translated from French by Donald Nicholson-Smith. New York: Zone Books.

Derrida, Jacques. 1978. The Theater of Cruelty and the Closure of Representation. In *Writing and Difference*, translated from French by Allan Bass. London and New York: Routledge & Kegan Paul.

Fischer-Lichte, Erika. 2004. *Ästhetik des Performativen*. Frankfurt/M: Suhrkamp.

Freud, Sigmund. 1982. Die Zukunft einer Illusion. In *Studienausgabe, Vol. IX. Fragen der Gesellschaft*. Frankfurt/M: S. Fischer.

Groys, Boris. 2003. *Topologie der Kunst*. Munich: C. Hanser.

Heidegger, Martin. 1961. *Nietzsche I–II*. Pfullingen: G. Neske.

———. 1977. *Vier Seminare*. Frankfurt/M: V. Klostermann.

———. 1983. Die Herkunft der Kunst und die Bestimmung des Denkens. In *Distanz und Nähe: Reflexionen und Analyse zur Kunst der Gegenwart*, ed. Petra Jaeger and Rudolf Lüthe. Würzburg: Königshausen & Neumann.

———. 1985. *Nietzsche: Der Wille zir Macht als Kunst*. Gesamtausgabe: II. Abteilung. Vorlesungen 1923–1976, Vol. 43. Frankfurt/M: V. Klostermann.

———. 2000. Die Frage nach der Technik. In *Vorträge und Aufsätze*, GA. Vol. 7. Frankfurt am Main: V. Klostermann.

Henri-Lévy, Bernard. 2005. *Sartre: Der Philosoph des 20. Jahrhunderts*. Translated from French to German by Petra Willim. Munich: Deutscher Taschenbuch Verlag.

Johnston, Adrian. 2006. Ghosts of Substance Past: Schelling, Lacan, and the Denaturalization of Nature. In *LACAN: The Silent Partners*, ed. Slavoj Žižek, 34–55. London and New York: Verso.

Kamper, Dietmar, and Christa Wolf, eds. 1981. *Die Wiederkehr des Körpers*. Frankfurt/M: Suhrkamp.

———, eds. 1982. *Das Schwinken der Sinne*. Frankfurt/M: Suhrkamp.

Kojève, Alexandre. 1980. *Introduction to the Reading of Hegel.* Translated from French by James H. Nichols, Jr. Ithaca and London: Cornel University Press.

Lacan, Jacques. 1966. Kant avec Sade. In *Écrits.* Paris: Seuil.

———. 1986. *Le Seminaire Livre VII: L'Ethique de la psychoanalise.* Text établi par J.-A. Miller, 2nd ed. Paris: Seuil.

———. 1991. *The Seminar of Jacques Lacan. Book II: The Ego in Freud's Theory and in the Technique of Psychoanalysis: 1954–1955.* Translated from French by Tomaselli Sylvana. New York: W.W. Norton & Company.

———. 2001. *Autre Écrits.* Paris: Seuil.

———. 2004. *The Four Fundamental Concepts of Psychoanalysis.* Translated from French by Alan Sheridan. London and New York: Routledge.

———. 2013. *On the Names-of-the-Father.* Translated from French by Bruce Fink. Cambridge: Polity Press.

Lemaire, Anika. 1977. *Jacques Lacan.* 8th ed. Sprimont: Mardaga.

Lipovetsky, Gilles. 2006. *Le bonheur paradoxal. Essai sur la société d'hyperconsommation.* Paris: Gallimard.

Lüdeking, Karl Heinz. 1994. Zwischen den Linien: Vermutungen zum aktuellen Frontverlauf im Bilderstreit. In *Was ist ein Bild?* ed. Gottfried Boehm, 344–365. Munich: W. Fink.

Lüthy, Michael. 2005. Relationale Ästhetik: Über den 'Fleck' bei Cézanne und Lacan. In *Blickzähmung und Augentäuschung: Zu Jacques Lacans Bildtheorie,* ed. Claudia Blümle and Anne von Heiden, 265–288. Zürich and Berlin: Diaphanes.

Manovich, Lev. 2001. *The Language of New Media.* Cambridge, MA, London and New York: The MIT Press.

Mirzoeff, Nicholas, ed. 2002. *The Visual Culture Reader.* London and New York: Routledge.

Ons, Silvia. 2006. Nietzsche, Freud, Lacan. In *LACAN: The Silent Partners,* ed. Slavoj Žižek, 79–89. London and New York: Verso.

Paić, Žarko. 2007. *Event and Emptiness: The Essays on the End of History.* Zagreb: Antibarbarus Editieons.

———. 2008. *Visual Communication: An Introduction.* Zagreb: Center for Visual Studies.

Reckwitz, Andreas. 2008. *Subject.* Bielefield: Transcript.

Rilke, Rainer Maria. 2014. *Duino Elegies.* Translated from German by Edward Snow. New York: North Point Press.

Sartre, Jean-Paul. 1960. *Critique de la raison dialectique: Précede de Question de la méthode.* Vol. I. Paris: Gallimard.

Sloterdijk, Peter. 1983. *Kritik der zynischen Vernunft.* Vol. I–II. Frankfurt/M: Suhrkamp.

———. 1986. *Der Denker auf der Bühne: Nietzsche Materialism.* Frankfurt/M: Suhrkamp.

Sutlić, Vanja. 1987. *The Practice of Labor as Scientific History: Historical Thinking as Criticism of the Crypto-Philosophical Structure of Marx's Thought.* 2nd ed. Zagreb: Globus.

Zima, Peter V. 2007. *Theorie des Subjekts: Subjektivität und Identität Zwischen Modern und Postmodern.* 2nd ed. Tübingen and Basel: A. Francke.

Žižek, Slavoj. 1989. *The Sublime Object of Ideology.* London and New York: Verso.

———. 1992. *Looking Awry: An Introduction to Jacques Lacan through Popular Culture.* Cambridge, MA, London and New York: The MIT Press.

———. 2000. *The Ticklish Subject.* London: Verso.

———. 2006a. *LACAN: The Silent Partners.* London and New York: Verso.

———. 2006b. *The Parallax View.* Cambridge, MA and London: The MIT Press.

4

Anti-philosophy of Immanence

4.1 Introduction

In the text dealing with body-language analysis in the thinking of contemporary French philosopher Pierre Klossowski, author of one of the best Nietzsche studies in the French language by any means, Gilles Deleuze argued that "in a certain way our era reveals perversion" (Deleuze 1993: 341). At the time of the Marquis de Sade, perversion had a subversive function of demolishing the moral law. When the "unnatural" is symbolically cleansed as "natural", then within the area of the "naturalness" of sexual intercourse between humans, perversion is something other than in our epoch. Deleuze points to this essential difference. It is pervaded, by him, with being called only what is precisely the objective power of showing, which makes it possible to distinguish between two orders of nature–morality. If for Klossowski there is no obscenity per se, it designates the entry of the body into a flaw in the language through which the language transcends its spoken situation by reflection on the body itself, when the experience of transgression in the language has been located in the language itself. So the language that enables awareness to

© The Author(s) 2019
Ž. Paić, *White Holes and the Visualization of the Body*,
https://doi.org/10.1007/978-3-030-14467-8_4

be raised to the level of reflection on obscurity must be rooted in the body as the boundary between what the body expresses as somatic and, in turn, what the body says semiotically. This paradoxical presence/absence of language in the body and the body in language comes to reality in the act of perverted pleasure. That is why Deleuze could make the point that the second discovery of our epoch should be the discovery of theology (Deleuze 1993: 342).

There is no longer a necessity to believe in God at all, Deleuze says, because there is a search for the structure or form of the testimony of religious beliefs and not true religious feeling. Though the latter view is only a modernized statement of the dispute between Christian theology as a "Christian philosophy" and a metaphysical tradition from which it is precisely performed by a second-rate scholarly faith, and not the philosophical question of divine meaning in the world, it is noticeably more challenging to think. Deleuze in the context of reading the assumptions of Klossowski's citation of Gombrowicz's novel *Pornography* comes to the key assumption of his entire thinking of the contemporary world as "bodies without organs". Indeed, theology in this sense becomes a substitute for knowledge of God, or, better, that knowledge is non-existent in reality. Language conquers this empty place of theology that no longer thinks of God in his metaphysical openness as a Being. On the contrary, theology might be placed in dysfunctional language itself. Hence, Klossowski, according to Deleuze, has rightly come to the standpoint of the perversion of the body towards the power of reflecting theology related to the world as such (Deleuze 1993: 342). The unity of theology and pornography is therefore not a stumbling block to the destruction of the idol of Christianity with the figure of the Antichrist. This designates a structural unity of dysfunction. Perversion, as well as theology, is a dysfunctional means of body-language experience in the contemporary cultural visual fascination with the body as a picture.

Both discoveries of our epoch are actually the uncanny subject to something beyond pornography as the linguistic-visual event of the world in its dysfunction. So perversion lies in the body language of the body without a spiritual substance, and theology is a substitute speech about God as a non-essential relationship to *things*. The perverse-theological turn of our epoch, radicalizing Deleuze's fundamental idea of his anti-philosophy, is that the experience of pornography has led to the limitations of the disappearance of the body itself into the total body of the world at large.[1] How could this be possible and what is meant by the accepted, but at the same time completely unreflected on, syntagm of Deleuze about the *body without organs*? The body disappears into the total body of the world as pornography of the world just because it is exhausted with what the body allows to be the body and what the body allows the body to have. The body without organs is, finally, the result of the ontological dysfunction of language itself that transforms itself into a thing by becoming an experience of perversion and theology of the language-in-body itself. When the body disappears in a pure visual fascination with the body-image, then it is exhausting that the language opens up a new horizon of world meaning. The language is not an organ, nor a substance. Quite analogously, the body would not be a subject or a Lord in his own house, if we might repeat what Lacan says about the position of the subject in a new world. Hence, the relationship between language and body is an analogous relationship that in traditional philosophy as in metaphysics belongs to the relation of the Being and beings.

4.2   Deleuze and the Body as a Desiring Machine

Language designates a condition of corporeal speech and is going on in the absence of articulated language. When the body "shuts" it talks with another apparatus of a "language game", just like gesture and reflexive mimicry. In this regard, the issue that Gilles Deleuze's view opens of inevitably contemplating the very contemporaneity in the gaps of empathy, communication, visual and body is therefore not just set in a new context of old concepts. It might be a question of a structural and formal condition under which one can still speak of the world without the horizons of its meaning. Or, put in other words, it is a question of the dysfunctional nature of the reduced world and of the logic of the rule of global capital as a universal "desiring machine". The change in the way of speaking about the life of this essentially dysfunctional world testifies that the language in which the modern world is described is an ontological perversion:

its posture corresponds to the theological posture of body language in the situation of the principal transgression of all moral-political prohibitions. The science of God deals with the body as an object because it has itself been expelled from the centre of speech about the subject. God in the dysfunction of the world inhabits bodies available as objects of lust. The other can no longer be a "subject" that forever guarantees the meaning of this world. It is its "function" that in the universal perversion of the world what might be ultimately accomplished from the transcendental grid makes sense: that, in fact, acts as a *thing* or as a *thing-in-itself* (*an-sich*).

In all the movies that deal with perverted sexual relations and project them into the social and ideological-political problems of our epoch, such as masterpieces of the problem of the relationship between the villain and the victim, the totalitarian Nazi regime and its disobedience of the reign of sexual perversion, and after the end of totalitarianism as a political-ideological system, as could be determined from the film by Lilliane Cavani, *The Night Porter* with Dirk Bogarde and Charlotte Rampling, what always remains behind that pornographic–obscene in the body is somewhat uncannily sublime. What remains is a *matter* that produces perversion and simultaneously can be sprinkled in the language. How is it doing this and under which conditions? First of all, the production and degeneration of *things* are sublime by the loss of the metaphysical rank of the world itself. The poststructuralist theory of the subject therefore inevitably starts from this condition. If that could not be disputable, then we are faced with an obvious paradox: When language no longer speaks about that primordial trauma, who else can be a witness to this uncanny "ontological perversion" except the image, which contains some elementary lack in its determination? Namely, the image in the form of the picture is always a sign of something already being done as being there.

Anyway, the language spoken by the subject is the "thing" that, when it is no longer behind but "there", as Lacan determined the change of image function in modern painting, is referred to by the body in its perverted-theological narratives of sexuality. Pornography without God has represented the same as the visual fascination of orgasmic performance in *white holes*. Emptying things leads to the disappearance of the very *thing* that gives meaning to the sexual act. The established language in the significant rule of difference gains its identity by being reduced to visual communication between bodies-images as objects of desire. The machine-calculated language of the new media, as the German visual theoretician of new media Friedrich A. Kittler has accurately described, corresponds to the idea of changing the language of the contemporary world, which has become a picture of bodies without organs (Deleuze and Guattari 1972). Most noteworthy, that syntagm conceals all that is the result of the emptiness of the contemporary world in its realization of Western philosophy as metaphysics. In the "heart" of *axiomatic capitalism itself*, there is a turning point. It is no longer machines of ideas that work behind things, but a materialistic realization of the desire of itself, not the pleasure of itself, in the space–time zone of the machine itself. That zone is free of territory. It has a new code that registers the "sensitive logic". In that sense, the mathematical structure of capitalism seems quite identical to the binary code that establishes virtual reality.

Instead of a transcendental source of the idea that allows beings to appear, instead of its structural-formal ontological primacy of the original, the body without organs designates the ultimate immanence of image–body–things. From this kind of turn, which can be more of a turnaround to the body, Deleuze, in the distant past of the entire philosophical aesthetic tradition, which has been maintained to date in the phenomenological approach to art (Merleau-Ponty and Lacan with a psychoanalytic addition), follows something almost identical to Malevich's first *Manifesto of Suprematism*. Namely, art does not reflect the appearance and relationship of the subject and object of painting. The image that emerges from the image of the body itself in its immanence without a superior source is attributed to the affect and nervous system, feeling and sensitivity, the logic of sensation, not the metaphysics of representation.[2] Already in his first decisive paper on the overall "new" orientation of poststructuralism entitled *Nietzsche and Philosophy*, Deleuze has taken on the problem of overcoming the dialectical understanding of the rule of the mind in all of history (Deleuze 1962).[3] The true alternative to Hegel's dialectics has found the difference in life itself in its fragmentation. Immanence has become, all the way, the key moment in overcoming the entire history of dialectics with its transcendental structure of thoughts "from above". It is a turning point towards the body in its sense, the logic of sensation, the final result of Deleuze's anti-philosophy. So the body has been located and represented in its present Being as its openness in the world, just like a place of the radical turn of metaphysics.

However, the concept that Deleuze introduces as an alternative to the reign of the mind carries a term well known from the ancient ontological tradition—*immanence* (Günzel 1998: 12). This is not a simple contrast to transcendence. Descent, metaphorically speaking, from Heaven to Earth does not mean setting the lower one to the rank of the upper. The distinct concept of Being as being, according to Nietzsche's view, is here elaborated in the context of "territorial processes" within clinical methods of treating psychopathological phenomena. In analogy, the analysis of the schizophrenia of capitalism, the undermining of the notion of its multi-plication in the formal and content sense of the impossibility of the fixed identity of a person, leads to such a turn that corresponds to the philoso-phy of immanence. It is crucial to consider the theme of the body itself in this production of doubled identities. Deleuze and Guattari have therefore introduced into *Anti-Oedipus* the syntagm body without organs by Antonin Artaud. The function of this concept is quite specific: the definition of immanent forms of life that are "postmetaphysical" in their utterly social functionalization within the language and communi-cation that operate the social sciences and humanities. The form of life that is paradigmatic in all social and clinical transformations is the figure of the masochist.

Deleuze and Guattari quote Artaud from *Theater of Cruelty*:

> The body is the body. Alone it stands. And in no need of organs. Organism it never is. Organisms are the enemies of the body. (Deleuze and Guattari 1987: 59)

For Deleuze and Guattari in Artaud's programmatical approach to his theatre of cruelty, the emphasis is not on the body against organs as such in the sense of the integrity of the body itself, but in the rejection of the "organic organization of organism". Medically, the body is not accessed as the whole of the spiritual properties of the organism, but as a functional part. The body in relation to its transcendence, which traditionally favours its meaning, escapes into the imminent complex. Organic in the organism as a system is not "naturally" organic, it should be a result of a modern articulation of science that breaks it alive from a scientific understanding of life. The biological notion of life is not the original concept of life. In his analysis of the history of institutional oversight of bodies through the biopolitical production of knowledge about the body, Michel Foucault directed critical attention to this.

The step towards what Deleuze thinks of as the very immanence of the body in its anti-philosophy is precisely to break down the original and postmetaphysical concept of life. The body cannot be otherwise placed in the centre of contemporary thinking without deconstructing the very notion of life. The body acquires its integrity in opposing the organism, so that the "living body" is somewhat different from the "living body" of a contemporary scientific approach to life. But as in Artaud's theatre of cruelty the mysticism of life's originality did not assume the modern existence of life itself, but from the time the ecstasy of the future meant life in its inexhaustible life, so Deleuze does not start from the already constant being that the body without organs guarantees existence. The essence is being divided into life itself in its singular event, and the body is not overwhelming, but always restructured. The body, therefore, becomes itself through a complex configuration of the relationship to the magma, not beyond oneself, but in the here and now, within the body's own life.

The body without organs belongs, finally, to the body's structure. When we say that it is a structure, it should be recalled that Heidegger's destruction of the fundamental ontology has the main intention of overcoming all metaphysical binary oppositions. The essence of Being and God as the essence is always thought of from this structure, always starting from the essence of Being. The organization of metaphysics states that the ontological difference between the Being and the being derives from the fracture within the original openness of the Being. But that fracture is not the same as Lacan assumes in his theory of a decentered subject, which goes between the imaginary and symbolic organization of the subject. The craze/gaze with which the fundamental structure of metaphysics is concerned is not "visible". It might be invisible and speechless, but it should be "seen" and "heard" within the body's own openness during its historical event. Understanding the body epochally means always starting with its contingency. Mortality as the ultimate limit of the body designates only the mortality of the being.

Heidegger has placed a man in the area of being there (*Dasein*) with the body which he "carries" and "holds" because he is a mortal being who through the experience of the body has an ontological difference between Being and beings. Bodily experience, therefore, cannot signify the empirical gift of the existence of man in the human body, which differs from all other living beings and their bodies; in the existential experience of death, it determines its being aware of its own ultimate existence. No doubt, it is quite clear that French structuralists and poststructuralists, as well as postmodernists (Lacan, Deleuze, Derrida, Foucault, Lyotard, Baudrillard), came to this problem of the body and existence through Kierkegaard and Nietzsche in their critique of Hegel's dialectics. What is, however, crucial here is that the organization of metaphysics has a strong internal structure. This means that the unceasing horizon of bodily thinking might be precisely what has been emphasized as the underlying problem of overcoming Hegel's dialectic since Nietzsche. Namely, it should be a question of whether the singularity of being in the very existence of the body as a living experience has represented an alternative to Hegel's thinking of the Being in the totality of the absolute spirit. The question is about reaching the final border, but only in the overall intentions of Deleuze in his anti-philosophy as in the wake of the body without organs. Rather, it might also be the entire anti- or postmetaphysical philosophy which after Lacan has constantly returned to the new founding of the subject. Can anybody, then, be an entity without a body that is "not" contingent, but becomes a body only in the singularity through language as the horizon of the world in which it and such a body "lives there" with the experience of temporality? Finally, does not the origin of the word used by Heidegger for the means of historical metaphysics—*Verfassung* (Heidegger 1959)—just designate the structure which should be related to what is the basic idea of structuralism: namely, whether it is a logical-historical arrangement or a structuring of the world as a machine?

Organisms and organs are by no means mechanically opposed to organic, artificial or "dead" versus the living "organization" of the organism. Artaud's pronouncement of the body without organs in Deleuze's immanence must, therefore, be understood in the attempt to distract from Hegel's dialectics of the absolute spirit. In the second part of the *Science of Logic*, Hegel says:

> The whole is not an abstract unity, but unity as a *differentiating manifold*; but this unity as one that is *multi actually* related is the *determinate* of what that part is. (Hegel 1986: 169)

Is this place of totality not at the same time a signpost for the entire path of deconstruction of the subject in the anti- or postmetaphysical philosophy of Lacan? The problem with which only Heidegger was obviously seriously faced, although not through Kierkegaard and Nietzsche but in his own understanding of the temporality of the Being, was and remains unresolved. The setting for an ineffective whole or a false entity, or whether Hegel's thought of totality sacrificed the "subject" and its existence in the name of the system, in no case is "true" even when Hegel's constructive and Marx's destructive dialectics are deconstructed in such a way that man is dislodged to the parts, organs and assemblies of something "imminently". Surprisingly, therefore, it might not be an abstract unity, but a living manifold of difference. What determines the whole in its integrity does not come from parts or from something beyond parts, but comes over the parts. It is a transcendental unity or being alone for the wholeness of life as an idea of life.

No doubt, Heidegger could never separate himself from the magical embrace of Hegel as the supreme metaphysics, precisely because he saw the truly irremediable throughout Hegel's mind. It is true, though, that it shows its "relativism" in parts of the whole, but not as the relative truth or truth of the part to the account of the whole, but as incomplete or incomplete in its development of absoluteness. All Heidegger's categories in his entire thinking were therefore derived in an analogy with the view of the integrity of the whole and of the metaphors of physical organization as an onto-theological structure (Being-God). There is a man in opposition to his anthropological attachment to the subject (Sutlić 1988). This is the fundamental difference between Heidegger and Lacan. Thus, it is a completely unfounded narrative, which Žižek tries to prove, that the problem of language that Heidegger calls the horizon from which the meaning of the Being in Lacan derives is deepened by the fact that the language in its body (the world of body language) is the traumatic experience of sacrifice (giving and rendering sacrifice, as in the case of Antigone; Žižek 2000).

The "proactive" action in the giving of a Being such as the victim of the "subject" (= words or language) that becomes the body goes towards the "passive" event of the incarnation of language without the victim of the "subject" being reduced to the same. But what is not the same is that it is in language that I allow the so-called subject to become a "subject" of speech, not vice versa. In language, the meaning and meaninglessness of the world are happening, and what should be said to the first person of a single narrative about the world is that is my daily way of expressing the truth about it, but Heidegger in the existential organization of *Sorge* as nursing lashed the Being itself from beingness, the essence of (man) and time, performed quite a different path of thinking. If language should be able to be a condition of unconsciousness, which is Lacan's unrivalled assumption, who then speaks to who in the being of language: the subject to the language that allows it or the language to the subject that is enabled in the language? Between the language and the world, obviously, there exists an uncanny abyss.

The subject's thinking as an unconscious articulation of language in the symbolic horizon of the world assumes this fracture, but leaves it untouched. Language as a body of a subject—Lacan's predicament— therefore tells the traumatic truth of one's own sacrifice to become a "person" or a subject in a decentered sense of the Lord without a Master. But this language of the subject should represent an unconscious articulation of what Lacan leaves in the metaphysical tradition as very unattractive. Of course, this must be the language of the unconscious *it* or, if not that, *one thing*. How could we be able to explain that thought operation which implicitly has far-reaching consequences for the notion of the body in our digital mediascapes? Obviously, the anthropological horizon is nothing other than the deprivation of the whole, or, even better, the imperfection of every subject's thinking with the paradigmatic case of the theoretical psychoanalysis of Freud–Lacan, because in its return to Descartes and Hegel, they do so only from the same starting point, which is already at the very beginning inadequately denied: that is, man is a "subject", a structural network of relationships or an intersubjective relationship between phenomena and things, as in Flusser's media theory. Any thinking of the body from that perspective can only fall below the level of Hegel, for whom anthropology and "soul" issues—independently of psychoanalysis, the "soul" is treated more complexly in the notion of the unconscious subject—are absorbed within the subjective spirit, the lowest stage in self-observation of the Absolute. A man can "have" a body only when he lays down his life and owns "his" being as his existential project. In Artaud's words, not knowing or unconsciousness, but just life–self-determination of life, decides on the nature of the existential project that is truly open.

In which way does Deleuze evaluate Hegel's dialectics? How did he come to the immanence of bodies without organs as a modern alternative to the psychoanalytic notion of the unconscious (Lacan)? Does Deleuze think that the logic of sensation is a true image of art at all in its dealing with the body beyond the mechanical organization of the world as a body? Let us anticipate Deleuze's conclusion before we point out the direction of thinking, the underlying category, and the way of articulating a completely different understanding of the subject in the contemporary world of visualization of the body. In the world of bodies without organs, there is no longer any reason to talk about culture at all. As Baudrillard pointed out in his analysis of *Crash* and so went further than Deleuze himself in contemplating the consequences of his settings, when man no longer desires (erogenous zones) in a purely visual fascination with the machine itself as an object (car and highway like the metaphors of the contemporary world of objects), then there is no culture or value any more. The empathy of the meaning of the world finishes/ends in bodies without organs or in the pure visualization of the deterritorialized world as an image. It is no longer the result of the act of the subject. But it is no longer an object (readymade) from the surrounding world. Let us make this last step in completing the world as an inter-communicative body that no longer applies to society or to culture. Did life for Artaud, and Deleuze and Guattari, not become a biotechnological machine without desire, the clean surface, the whiteness of the white holes in the Being itself? Is it truly possible with Deleuze to save some more aesthetics of sensation, sensuality, ecstatic pleasure of the body in the new concept of art, as many contemporary body theorists want as images (Grosz 2008)?

Deleuze and Guattari in *Anti-Oedipus* and *A Thousand Plateaus*, in the first part of *Capitalism and Schizophrenia*, develop two key concepts of their theory of culture: (1) desiring machines, and (2) bodies without organs. It should be said at the outset that these are not just concepts opposed to the traditional notion. In the first, there is no mere contrast to "soul machines", for example; and in the second, there is no contrast to the mechanically produced body as an organism. It is possible to accept the assertion of Stephan Günzel, a German interpreter of Deleuze, that both of these concepts are common to their dissolution of the Western theological tradition. Within its frame, the soul was perceived immortally and beyond the borders of worldliness. The body without organs might, therefore, be free from the "soulless" body; that is, this soul who has been cast out of the body as a superhuman's aura performed by the theological tradition. The body cannot return its dignity, its original freedom, without the resurgence of the metaphysical tradition in which it was imprisoned. So the desiring machine and the body without organs are seemingly "robotized" concepts of the total human posture. But in the situation of developed capitalism as a socio-communicative system of perverse realization of the human in things, schizophrenia surely designates a way of existence which is fragmented in identity.

Lust as an urgent and culturally mediated symbolic line of Western history is a machine-based, institutional (organic) system of all relationships between people in the territorial and temporal sequence of events. So organs without a body represent desiring machines assembled for the life in which the "soul" is seized to gain the true life of the body in freedom from the soul's bondage. Nietzsche's influence on Deleuze was, undoubtedly, decisive. Indeed, Nietzsche was a turning point in connection with Hegel's and Marx's dialectics in the whole of Deleuze's thinking. That is the reason why his and Guattari's criticism of psychoanalysis must be understood by a programme for analysis of the contemporary body. Culture represents the order of the perverted power system, not the original desire to overcome the contradictions of mind and body, of the Other, going beyond the boundaries of Being and of value. It can be said that Deleuze's "philosophy of immanence" represented a radical step in the deconstruction of the modern world, which has become exactly what it has been since the new era: to become a desiring machine programmed to a new will as an objective store of history comprehended just like memories, as well as a pure visualization of reality in numbers, images and words.

Deleuze and Guattari, in the traces of Artaud, are trying to perform a radical turn from psychoanalysis. This does not mean its negation. After all, we saw that Artaud with Freud had a touch in the way of dream interpretation as the basis of the imaginary field. Art lies in the "heart of darkness" of the imaginary. That is why it could be a turn from something (Freud and Lacan) to get something to do. Obviously, it could not be, therefore, a radical turn of thought, but a turning away to Nietzsche/ Artaud's return related to the primordial essence of life as "the unknown game of God and pleasure". Psychoanalysis designated for the philosopher Deleuze and the psychiatrist Guattari a modern form of Socrates' enlightenment: to know yourself by unconsciously awakening at the end of the session with the help of the Other (psychoanalysts). Instead, the schizo-analysis of the "desiring machine", as named in *Anti-Oedipus*, was represented by the direction of overcoming subjectivization completely. How could that be exactly done and with what kind of argumentation?

Deleuze and Guattari speak of five forms of bodies that are transformed and opposed by their subject in their unorganized bodies: (1) hypochondriac, (2) paranoid, (3) the schizo-body, (4) the body in a drugged condition, and (5) a masochistic body. At first glance, in the shift from the concept of "soul" (*psyché*), which operates in the psychoanalysis of Freud–Lacan with an emphasis on the formation of the subject as individual consciousness, and which is the decentered centre in the language as a symbolic horizon of the world, Deleuze and Guattari introduce a schizo-analytic alternative to psychoanalysis. A radical step or a return to the body is going back to the heart of darkness—a scattered and multiplied subject that has no fixed base. Finally, did not Lacan himself describe the position of a subject who is no longer a Master in his own house? It would be naïve immanence if it was simply about rejecting a theologically "ruined" notion of the soul over the world by its plague in the body as a "prison" of the world beyond. The schizo-analysis in *Anti-Oedipus* and *A Thousand Plateaus* assumes the results of a psychoanalytic theory of the subject. But they are not considered a solution to the fundamental problem: how to overcome the dichotomy of Western metaphysics as a culture of rationalizing–subjecting man. At the height of late or global capitalism, the disintegration of the metaphysical framework of the Being, beings and the essence of the human leads to the implosion of frenzy, or the dissolution of the identity of society, culture and life itself. In *Anti-Oedipus* and *A Thousand Plateaus*, the interlocutor and authority in this regard are certainly Foucault, and meta-criticism has been directed to Lacan and theoretical psychoanalysis. The five forms in which corporeal bodies without organs are happening are as follows:

1. The hypochondriac body experiences the body itself in the exclusion of deconstructions of the organs, in the medical sense of the creation of their destruction. In the assemblage of the mind, not having decided itself, because it does not exclude itself, hypochondria is always unable to touch what enables it. The body of hypochondria is, therefore, "embedded in purity" as the absurdity of the absoluteness in itself. It knows this by not knowing that the purity of absolute absolutes should be the illusion and fiction of the "subject" of such a body.

2. The paranoid body is taken in a concrete case by the president of the court of Daniel Paul Schreiber and his autobiography, which Sigmund Freud took for the paradigm of paranoia interpretation. It is a body that is perceived as a mirror of the outside world. Any information from that external world in the character order is recorded on the body itself. It serves as a one-off record of all social disturbances in the labelling sequence. Deleuze and Guattari in *Anti-Oedipus* almost equalize paranoia and schizophrenia.

3. The schizo-body is a reversed paranoid body; that is, the *desiring machine*. Hence, we can only ask a question about Kant's *thing-in-itself*. If schizophrenia is a "universal producer", as Deleuze and Guattari have said, then it might be in a world that has already changed so that the binary opposition of man and nature disappears. Being should be a procession. Man and nature do not exist "in-itself"; they are always processing placed in real-world events. Schizophrenic machines are made for lust, not a man, who is the object of lust in the

"nature" of the outside world. Therefore, in contrast to the transcendence of the paranoid body, which is set in the idealization of that I as someone else behind, the schizophrenic process of objectification might be located in pure immanence. Stepping back to this condition must be experimenting with a body that crosses its own immanent limits by taking drugs.

4. The body in a drugged condition as an "experimental schizo" is just an extreme case of superposition of the subject; that is, schizophrenia in the state of the medial process of "self" delivery. Drugs for such a body represent a substitute for a substance that allows it to move to the state of consciousness beyond the ego (subject). Artaud's writings about the magical function of peyote in *Tarahumara* meticulously literarily processed this "transition" from I to *that* which carries *I*. The mystical experiences of surpassing that somatic-semiotic in the body in the direction of ascension towards heaven are known in all the religious traditions of the world. But that does not mean that the body has lost the "ground under the feet" and has become a spiritual substance, rather than having the drugs gained for some other purpose. It is still the causal logic of the body's actions in the world. In experimental form, this designates the case of bodies without organs. Schizophrenia in a drugged condition corresponds to the social model of capitalism as a desiring machine. It has beyond and behind nothing but what it is in reality—production for another circle of production. There is a solution to the myth of the causality of man and nature in the process of an event of one and the same. The thing is, in fact, that the desiring machine might be inevitable like a fragmented thing—man/nature, body/soul, mind/feeling—which has its "mystical" nature in that the world without mystics becomes somewhere beyond its "social nature". What does a desiring machine want and why? The body without organs is craving for the organism of its own cleavage. To a self-evident "perfection" as the continuous circle of one and the same body without an organ belongs a state that is neither conscious nor unconscious.

The condition is a vital self-affirmation of a fundamental perversion of the world in language horizon narratives. Capitalism in that state represents the schizo-body of social relations. In them, man does not appear to a man, but is in advance without substance and is de-subjected. It is a state of pure self-sufficiency of desire for desire. Deleuze and Guattari in their analysis have critically demonstrated the limits of psychoanalysis in the interpretation of the contemporary world. But they did not go beyond the framework of Marx's anthropological criticism of Hegel's Absolute. In other words, they did not deconstruct the fundamental assumption of Marx's destructive dialectics of capitalism that man is the embodiment of historically generated social relations. From structuralist theory, that simply could not be possible. The reason lies in the fact that social relations are considered within the network of structures and functions, the symbolic exchange of signs as the social networks of the signifier and the signified.

5. Why should it be so decisive for the overall analysis carried out in *Anti-Oedipus* and *A Thousand Plateaus* to understand the concept of the body without organs with the understanding of the masochistic body? Bringing pain on "your" body is not the goal of a subject in relation to the pain caused by someone else or himself. The masochist, according to Deleuze and Guattari, does not follow any fantasy, nor is it a mere contingency of pain on the body. The underlying disadvantage of the psychoanalytic interpretation of the masochistic body is that pain in the sense of self-perceiving pain should be considered as something transcendent. The experience of pain as a necessity for pleasure comes from psychoanalysis, from something beyond the body, which makes it enjoyable. In his approach to Nietzsche, in his first book Deleuze came to the solution of this philosophical, structural-ontological problem. Instead of the platonic duplication of the world, it should be, on the contrary, the materialistic turn of a subject to a body that is "there", not beyond. So no more can be said about a subject who unconsciously senses that the truth of his subjectivity *is it* behind the principle of pleasure. Thus, Deleuze and Guattari in this process of de-subjectivization within the masochistic body speak of events based on a refined concept from the scholastic theology of Duns Scotus' *haecceities*. It is a mutual play of reality and possibilities by which the principle of individuation allows the establishment of the subject (ego).

Masochism, therefore, is not interpreted psychoanalytically as somehow a psychopathological "tendency" to submit to unusual pain in increasing (the accumulation of) pleasure. It is something essentially different. Instead of staying in the dialectics of Lord–servant (sadism–masochism), it is necessary to go beyond this superordinating and submissive discourse of power. Masochism is analysed, paradoxically and only reasonably, in analogy with Hegel's dialect of Absolute History in which the true self-consciousness needs the being-subordination (servant) in an attempt to establish wholeness by the establishment of a new principle—economy or work as substance—as a subject of the advanced civil world. Masochism denotes a literary figure, but much more than a psychopathological form of apparent loss of the dignity of a person in exchange for the accumulated pleasure here, in this body, anywhere outside. When the victim speaks in the language of his torturer, then the phenomenon of the masochistic body must be radically different from Freud and psychoanalysis. For Deleuze, the essential difference between sadism and masochism is that in the opinion of sadism after de Sade there are two natures: primary and secondary. The latter is an immeasurable nature. It is an event of emergence and disappearance within it. But the emphasis is on the first nature as a pure negation. In its destructive attitude towards the body of the Other, it can never reach the state of final delight, but it is mediated by the absolute destruction of the body of the Other. Sadism in this primordial form is possible only as the absolute creation of the Being (or Other). In its destructive attitude towards the body of the Other, it can never reach the state of final delight, but is mediated by the absolute destruction of the body of the Other.

What represents the problem of this destructive–constructive dialectic of history that determines the entire culture of capitalism as a structural way of producing "desiring machines"? Hegelian says, and this is only an overturned form of Marx's position of historical materialism, that masochism signifies the true sadism. The sufferer encourages the tormenter by making the pleasure of suffering pain (suffering and overcoming pain with pleasure) to his awareness of the absolute destruction of the first and second nature. The proletariat is an in-itself of history as a revered masochistic machine of desire for the realization of sadism in his final "calm" by the disappearance of the difference between the torturer and the victim. Deleuze and Guattari have tried to establish a "distinctive dialectics" of history. This means that it is no longer possible to establish a new entity, because paradoxically it is possible only within the two-dimensional dialectics or the binary opposition of Lord–servant. When both members become abolished by servant becoming Lord, and slavery no longer has its substantive basis because the new Master is not at all a "master" but is to reverse the servant's history that has disappeared in processual unity, and the two members are gone, then the fundamental question might be: Who is at all the so-called subject of post-history? Deleuze's strategy in his anti-philosophy of immanence is ultimately philosophically strange. First of all, this is because he interprets the entire history of philosophy from the point of view of immanence as an orientation point of thought. His genetic method in the trajectory of Nietzsche is always diachronic-critical. This means that Spinoza, for example, opposes Descartes, Nietzsche to Kant, Bergson to Hegel and Sacher-Masoch to Freud, so that the concept of a body without organs opposes the idea of a mechanical organism, and a schizo-analysis of psychoanalysis, which is how Günzel correctly argued. Thus, such an interpretation does not exhaust itself in the hermeneutic circle of interpreting the text from the inside, for the very text of what is being interpreted becomes the basis of a new thinking. Finally, that immanence would oppose the unknowing transcendence.

What are the consequences of such an interpretation? Deleuze was justifiably attempting to undergo theoretical psychoanalysis for critical valuation in view of his starting position on the unconscious subject. The fact that the moment of "suppressing" that radically different course of history and shifting the focus to the other governing order of ideas, as is the case with Lacan's views on the decentered subject, already present in this position, appears to be Deleuze's most significant achievement in the method of thinking. Imagine the contemporary culture of the global kind of capitalism as a desiring machine that permeates the war machine as well as the machine of sexual perversions of order built on the ideological grounds of liberalism, which seems sufficiently stimulating for what should be the subject of this debate. We do not enter here extensively into exposing the difficulty of such a method. We only deal with what is evident in Deleuze's philosophical assumptions about the body without organs. Before we point out the consequences of such a criticism of the subject for the possibility of thinking in the second order of the meanings of the body as an image (the logic of sensation), we still need to remain a little longer on the differences between psychoanalysis, not so much in Freud's thinking but in Lacan's theory, and Deleuze and Guattari's schizo-analysis of the desiring machine of the contemporary visual culture of capitalism as the total machine of history.[4]

What exactly in the aforementioned *Anti-Oedipus* and *A Thousand Plateaus* Deleuze and Guattari do in this regard? Contrary to the psycho-analysis of Lacan, like Derrida, as we have shown in his interpretation of Artaud, they point to the reversal of the underlying psychoanalytic con-cept—unconsciously. Hence, the emphasis on the masochistic body might be the programmatic act of turning the signifier. Instead of Freud's formula of the goal of psychoanalysis, *Wo Es war, soll Ich werden* (Where it was, shall I be), which for Deleuze is proof of being unconsciously subjected to the ultimate reach of psychoanalysis, it is necessary to get out of the vicious cycle of the unconscious in the rupture of the language. This means that Deleuze deconstructs the method itself and the goal of psychoanalysis by observing it within the framework of the society of the control of the schizophrenia of capitalism. Anti-Oedipus is a reversed desiring machine that has lost its "idealistic" or transcendental lever to suppress the imaginary order of nature in the sublime order of the sym-bolic perversion of history. What needs to be reversed is just the funda-mental ontological principle of psychoanalysis—unconsciously.

This, of course, also reverses this new subject theory as the basis for a new visual culture of the contemporary world. What, then, instead of the unconscious? Nothing but the body as a desiring machine, and not lan-guage as a symbolic order of the unconscious. Against that "ideology of lack" which determines psychoanalysis, Deleuze and Guattari in *Anti-Oedipus* affirmed the logic of denying the institutional justification of new contradictions in understanding the binary oppositions of madness and rationality. Restoring the body without organs certainly cannot denote a return to something that already existed in history. Bodies with-out organs are a concept, not the real condition of things. Therefore, the method of philosophical interpretation of that might be always "subversive", related to the lack of discovery of the affects and logic of the heart. The sensitivity in the body itself corresponds to the concepts of "plateaus" rather than areas or higher levels. So the key terms of Deleuze's thinking, such as *nomadism, chaos, deterritorialization and reterritorialization, rhizome*, derive from the imminent disintegration of the binary oppositions which lie consciously and unconsciously in the tradition beyond what Merleau-Ponty is setting as an "observation" object in the surrounding world.

In *Logic of Sense* and *What Is Philosophy?* Deleuze introduces the path of understanding art as a set of perceptions and impacts. The sensation that makes the aesthetic framework is not separated, as in the can, from the mere sphere. The sublime which has been at the core of Kant's aesthetics, with the key term of surpassing the mental and sensitive contradiction of the inexpressibility of what is shown in the picture, is no longer a transcendental image. The logic of sense is, therefore, the "logic" which meaning no longer has to seek in language as a logically structured script outside the body, but only in its "heart". However, Deleuze does not rehabilitate this passive "mindset" against the mind in the sense of a reversed metaphysics, which presupposes the existence of the essence of a Being.

The image that is created by art in modern art since Cézanne, as Merleau-Ponty, Lacan and Heidegger have shown, is at the very heart of the world. In its body, the image opens up a new "perspective". The artist, with his complete mode of painting, swarms into it without the illusion of the perspective of the truth of the Being. The effects are not a passing emotion. Malevich proclaims in his *Manifesto of Suprematism* that avant-garde art as "pure sensitivity", in the dimensions of an image that no longer fascinates the external "story", must be immanent in its essence of images without the world. The artwork for Deleuze hence designates the new, the created and, which is now only significant, is no longer related to the intention and the ambiguity of its creator. In this, human–inhuman distinctions disappear, because the artwork in its perceptual-affective self-affirmation of life flows above one and the Other. But it does so by not reconciling them, but rather opens them in the natural–human–inhuman opening of the body as image.

Deleuze's interpretation of the work of English painter Francis Bacon in *The Logic of Sensation* is probably one of the most significant philosophical studies of art after Merleau-Ponty's *Visible and Invisible* about Cézanne and Heidegger's study *On the Origin of the Work of Art* in which Van Gogh is discussed (Deleuze 2003). We can say that it is not a book about painting as the interpretation of one of the great modern twentieth-century painters. On the contrary, it is the study of the phenomenon of the aesthetic and artistic subject with philosophical insight into the essence of art in the age of the *corporeal turn*. What the body without organs in its "aesthetic-artistic" openness is can only be understood if, together with Bacon, we are able to abolish the distinction between figurative and abstract painting. In the second conceptual framework, it might be the omission of the distinction between transcendence and immanence.

For Deleuze, Bacon is a body sculptor without organs. His paintings are confirmed by the logic of sensation (fever as an incarnation) in processes of deterritorialization of machines of desire. This is already such an approach to painting that is placed in the "centre" by the body, in its somatic and semiotic sense, turning from previous phenomenological and bitter (hermeneutical) approaches to an artistic work (Cézanne–Van Gogh). There are three fundamental features that Deleuze shows in the entirety of Bacon's work:

1. destruction of a defined body,
2. taking the subject of artistic creation into the characters of the de-subjective human body from which the space of affectivity is produced (paradigmatic is the image of the *Screaming Pope*), and
3. the dynamics of being in procession.

Destruction, take-over and dynamism correspond to what Deleuze and Guattari developed in *Anti-Oedipus* and *A Thousand Plateaus*. The body is broken as an organism (a mechanical circuit) by opening the possibility of coming to the centre of the problem of artistic activity/events, the living affectivity of the artist in the "sensory logic". All this happens in the spatial and temporal pursuit of being the life of oneself. The bodies torn apart, laid in space, reduced to the body only, but not just to the "naked flesh", are placed in a body-image in which space only covers certain parts of the body.

This does not mean that Bacon prevails over anything from the tradition of the *corpus mysticum* of the sublime of the metaphysical and religious definition that the image depicts when it is explicitly "obeying" the spiritual in art. Bacon, quite the contrary, represents a picture in which a body without organs no longer belongs to gender/sex or any spiritual image of the body-image. It is the equality of the animal and the human. The body denotes a desiring machine independent of its "function" in the human–inhuman world. What Artaud wanted with his theatre of cruelty can be confirmed in Bacon's portraits. The body as an image does not represent a divine body. It is not the origin of the human body. Deleuze in Bacon's portraits sees the end of the idea of painting that shows what is inevitable. Lyotard followed Kant's thinking in these words defining the return of sublime in postmodernism (Lyotard 1988). The divine is, thus, no longer shown in the image. But there is no sign of any remaining trace. Instead, what the image is "showing" is, as Deleuze says, a different animal spirit of man. In a "spirit" identical to that of pigs, cattle, dogs, a man "lives" his physical adventure of life. But the word "spirit" no longer has the weight that all of metaphysical history carried of the structured language of differentiating humanity from the human being and the outside world in which animals live. If the body no longer resides in the human space of the "home of the subject", then it is thrown into another deterritorialized world. And that is where the space in the traditional understanding of that word really should be placed. Territories are not spaces. Body fatigue on "meat" corresponds to man's dependence on the thing. So Deleuze in the interpretation of Bacon's painting necessarily directs a self-contained attempt to show how the body without organs might be exposed in the image of artistic action/events:

> The body is the Figure, or rather the material of the Figure. The material of the Figure must not be confused with the spatializing material structure, which is positioned in opposition to it. The body is the Figure, not the structure. Conversely, the Figure, being a body, is not the face and does not even have a face. It does have a head because the head is an integral part of

the body. It can even be reduced to the head. As a portraitist, Bacon is a painter of heads, not faces, and there is a great difference between the two. For the face is a structured, spatial organization that conceals the head, whereas the head is dependent upon the body, even if it is the point of the body, its culmination. It is not that the head lacks spirit; but it is a spirit in bodily form, corporeal and vital breath, an animal spirit. It is the animal spirit of man: a pig-spirit, a buffalo-spirit, a dog-spirit (…). Bacon thus pursues a very peculiar project as a portrait painter: to dismantle the face. Body, Meat and Spirit to rediscover the head or make it emerge from beneath the face. (Deleuze 2003: 20)

The body in the somatic form of its existence is not mere "flesh". It is a desiring machine that dwells in the universe of the begotten creatures. Bacon as a portraitist no longer portrays "man" as such, nor the idea of man. The head is not the centre of spirituality, but what Deleuze accurately shows: the head designates the body of a deteriorated body of the body without organs. The inevitable consequence of this is not just the disappearance of the difference between man and animal, but an attempt to artificially open the possibility of overcoming abstract and figurative painting. Yet Bacon's painting belongs to the already significant transformation of the image into the body's own event. This completes the transition from the final to the infinite. This should be the decisive point of distinction between Deleuze and Heidegger. For the latter, it is a being in an uncanny existence of the man as being there (*Dasein*) in the Being-in-the-world. For Deleuze, who does not think from the position of the subject, the body cancels the distinction between man, animal and machine. But, of course, only the body is "without organs". Bacon's painting "shows" only conditionally this process of decomposition of transcendental image markers. Like Artaud, there is no longer a representative model of the image here. However, now the question should be asked of which model image Deleuze had in mind when he plunged into the "puzzle" of Bacon's *corporeal turn*. This obviously cannot be a communication model of the image, because bodies without organs are not inter-communicative bodies. Their only essence lies in the fascination of what Deleuze calls "the logic of sensation":

There are two ways of going beyond figuration (that is, beyond both the illustrative and the figurative): either toward abstract form or toward the Figure. Cézanne gave a simple name to this way of the Figure: sensation. The Figure is the sensible form related to a sensation; it acts immediately upon the nervous system, which is of the flesh, whereas abstract form is addressed to the head, and acts through the intermediary of the brain, which is closer to the bone. Certainly, Cézanne did not invent this way of sensation in painting, but he gave it an unprecedented status. The sensation is the opposite of the facile and the readymade, the cliché, but also of the "sensational," the spontaneous, etc. Sensation has one face turned toward the subject (the nervous system, vital movement, "instinct," "temperament" a whole vocabulary common to both Naturalism and Cézanne) and one face turned toward the object (the "fact," the place, the event). (Deleuze 2003: 34)

In one single place, in the book dedicated to Bacon's painting, Deleuze will explicitly say that the sensation is vibration. We leave a methodical speech about the so-called subject and the object to which the sensation sends its information without message through the artwork of the openness of bodies without organs. Then we are in doubt. Namely, the communication model of the image of the digital age as a paradigm of media visual culture no longer presents or represents. Such a model of the image is autoreferential and interrelated. The image is a calculated or technically produced image. Reality comes from its virtually irreplaceable nature, which distinguishes originals and copies. That is the reason why the image in the communication model should always be the result of the alignment of the picture with the body in its desired state of visual information about something real. The communication model of the image denotes only a socio-cultural manifestation of changes in ontological image status in the digital age. This image is computer modelled. Traditionally metaphysically speaking, it designates the essence of information that precedes any possible relationship between humans, animals and machines in a real–virtual community.

When Deleuze discerns the basic idea of "aesthetics" for the time of new media, which essentially ignores the distinction between the fields of "sensation" and "conceptualization", then the problem is that Bacon in figurative painting is just completing the radical idea of the historical avant-garde with Malevich as the starting point. This idea does not point to a change of society through the aesthetics of the world in which art becomes a socially engaged comment rather than a change of artistic art itself. The key to these changes, which are really a big turn, although no longer in the direction of the so-called subject ("artist" and his actions) but in the direction of the object (fact, place, event), is that the sensation entirely stems from the affection of the body itself in its singular event of time. The sensation or logic of feeling, which reminds us of the fractals of the "new aesthetics", can be nothing else but a performative-conceptual event of life itself in the pure body of events. It was the only place left in the field of contemporary art.

In the presence of real-time and virtual space, a visual fascination with the image of the body itself occurs. That is one reason why we cannot determine Deleuze's interpretation of a painting by Francis Bacon just as an illustration of his own philosophical preferences, but as an attempt to think of art at all in the contemporary world of the reign of desiring machines as the cinematic event of the body itself in its chaotic "nature". It should be not accidental that Slavoj Žižek in his book on Deleuze emphasized that the first determination of Deleuze's philosophy is that he was a "virtual philosopher", but also an "ideologist of digital capitalism" (Žižek 2003). However, these critical judgements were as provocative and quite failed, as well as him correctly pointing out that Deleuze did not radically break with Hegel's dialectics, but that these objections were guided by Lacan's theory of a decentered subject. Therefore, turning around bodies without organs cannot be thought of without radical criticism of the psychoanalytic theory of the subject. Deleuze's great innovation and at the same time somewhat questionable to the notion of the contemporary world is that, as a matter of fact, the whole poststructuralist theory has opened up the problem of overcoming the metaphysical oppositions of mind and body, and thus showed how much within the immanent space of the body it had already become the technological and postmetaphysical world of life.

The problem obviously could not be that Deleuze was merely a "virtual philosopher" or, according to the interpretation by Žižek, an "ideologist of digital capitalism", but that for the entire stated orientation of the subject's renewal and criticism (Lacan, Derrida, Foucault, Deleuze) something remained essentially unprepared. It might be precisely the area of determining the world in its horizon of meaning. However, it belongs to the transcendental status of capital as the *thing of* all possible sublime perversions in the real event of capitalism in the world.

4.3   Conclusion

The area critically analysed by Deleuze in the concept of a body without organs denotes a transformation of the very concept of man as a structural field of social relations. He may or can change with some conscious decision of a politically articulated subject—Badiou's "politics of truth" (Badiou 1998)—and so evolutionally turn the essence of the very transcendental horizon, or cannot be substantially changed by the "subject", but by the structural changes in social relations in their powerful objectivity. So Deleuze has indicated the problem of postulating the social relationships of a singular life. The body without organs, thus, does not represent a solution to the entire puzzle of history as self-awareness of the freedom of the original lifestyle. Bacon's painting was hence not paradigmatic for Deleuze to describe what is already the destiny of the world without "organs". On the contrary, the passage of the body outside of all inside and outside of the world into the "heart" of the deterritorialized world signifies a turning point towards what was at the beginning of the historical avant-garde in art an unprecedented assumption of the visualization of the world.

This assumption doubtless sounds sensational. Of course, this is, therefore, a structural field of pure sentiment versus Kant's intelligible sky of ideas. The feeling generated by art in the visual sense as vibration is not represented as a substitute for the sublime. Since the only thing left is the area of the head–body–image in the senses, which have the intellectual power of imagination (fantasy, *Einbildung*), then the fundamental question of turning contemporary art versus the head–body–image can be formulated with Deleuze in the following way: Why does the event of the contemporary world in real-time and virtual space still require a symbolic remaining body if it is already life itself beyond a body without organs? Why, then, does the body as an image disappear from the horizon of the world at all when it comes to emptying "desiring machines" in the pure pleasure of exchanging things for a thing? We have seen that Baudrillard in the analysis of David Cronenberg's film *Crash* laid the foundations for overcoming all "little narratives" of postmodernism and theories of *revival* subject to reaching the limitations of corporeality in the aestheticized "world" of the "love" and "death" of the body itself. The remaining areas of unresolved games are still just being emptied or emptied into the naked life of a biopolitical machine. But what is a biopolitical machine? Instead of the society and culture to which the signs of visualization of the world itself are related, as they lead to transparency, because both words are deprived of substantive meaning, such as information society and technological culture, is it paradoxical that only politics and its technological apocalyptic character are a condition of radical changes in life itself? But really, what kind of politics?

Notes

1. Baudrillard's approach to the end of sociability, image and contemporary art, which in its fascination with objects has since become the aestheticization of "objective reality", can be considered on the basis of the latest cybernetic (apocalyptic and neo-gothic) theories of the cyber-body to have already happened. Although it is not possible to draw directly the line that would entail the opinion of Deleuze and Baudrillard, since it is primarily a question of the correlation between paths of thought that are, of course, different, it is apparent that it is an insight of both thinkers that the period of radical corporeality of the world is a period of technological or media structuring of the realities of the body (Featherstone 2000).

2. Canadian theoretician of new media Arthur Kroker in his text on "desiring machines" and "body without organs" in Deleuze and Guattari's work *Anti-Oedipus* begins with the usual metaphors of *white walls* and *black holes*. The idea of a new kind of machine that goes beyond the anthropological issues of McLuhan's preference for man's attachment to his

technological body does not, according to Kroker, relate to new technology. Quite the contrary, it might be an analysis of the philosophical-social situation of the contemporary world in which the body is technologically completed in such a way that "the brain itself is decoded, the visions are decentered and philosophy is without a tradition for machine-made bodies without organs" (Kroker 1995).

3. Deleuze began his essay *Nietzsche and Philosophy* with a programmatic attitude about the game as differences in the forehead, which through the will to power can in a Nietzschean way establish a different understanding of contemporaneity than was the case in Hegel–Marx's confidence in the totality of mind. The radical step towards Nietzsche's horizons of the unknown "games, happiness, and God" did not only have a methodological and genealogical drive contrary to the subtraction of cognitive-living ground dialectics, but rather it was even a negative power in the sense of Adorno's version (the whole is false). Hence, it might be the opening of new possibilities to confirm what Nietzsche found in the primordial concept of the body—the feast of vitality, the sublimity of the body as a glimpse of all the pleasure and all the secret of openness of the Being in time (Paić 2007).

4. Deleuze's position in regard to Spinoza, namely a body without organs, was taken over by Antonio Negri's society of control of liberal-democratic postmodernism in a book written together with Michael Hardt entitled *Empire* (Hardt and Negri 2000). But the far more inspirational direction in the contemporary theoretical production of the analysis of body, machine, visual and spectacular global capitalism that surpasses all the differences of nature and culture can be found in the writings of Giorgio Agamben. In the concept of the *anthropological machine*, Agamben points out the distinction between man–animal, human–inhumane, because the anthropological machine works by excluding the "human" that was never "human", precisely because it was enframed as a value or as a culture. Thus, in the modern era, it is humanly animalized because it is humanly derived from the theory of evolution and the human being understood as a social organism (transferring Darwin's theory into the positivistic body of the organicism of sociology). Although Agamben returns to Foucault in his analysis of biopolitics and thinks of the trajectory of Heidegger, it is undeniable that he is closer to the ideas of Deleuze than to Foucault regarding this problem (Agamben 2004).

References

Agamben, Giorgio. 2004. *The Open: Man and Animal.* Translated from Italian by Kevin Attell. Stanford, CA: Stanford University Press.

Badiou, Alain. 1998. *Abrégé de métapolitique.* Paris: Editions du Seuil.

Deleuze, Gilles. 1962. *Nietzsche et la philosophie.* Paris: Press Universitaires de France.

———. 1993. *Logik des Sinns.* Translated from French to German by Bernhard Dieckmann. Frankfurt/M: Suhrkamp.

———. 2003. *Francis Bacon: The Logic of Sensation.* Translated from French by Daniel W. Smith. London and New York: Continuum.

Deleuze, Gilles, and Felix Guattari. 1972. *Anti-Oedipus.* Paris: Les Éditions de Minuit.

———. 1987. *Anti-Oedipus: Capitalism and Schizophrénia.* Translated from French by Robert Hurley, Mark Seem, and Helen R. Line. Minneapolis: University of Minnesota Press.

Featherstone, Mike, ed. 2000. *Body Modification.* London: SAGE.

Grosz, Elizabeth. 2008. *Chaos, Territory, Art: Deleuze and the Framing of the Earth.* New York: Columbia University Press.

Günzel, Stephen. 1998. *Immanenz: Zum Philosophiebegriff von Giles Deleuze.* Essen: Blau Eule.

Hardt, Michael, and Antonio Negri. 2000. *Empire.* Cambridge, MA and London: Harvard University Press.

Hegel, Georg Wilhelm Friedrich. 1986. *Wissenschaft der Logik.* Werke in 20. Bänden. Vol. 6. Frankfurt/M: Suhrkamp.

Heidegger, Martin. 1959. *Vorträge und Aufsätze.* Pfullingen: G. Neske.

Kroker, Arthur. 1995. Deleuze and Guattari: Two Meditations. [Online] Accessed November 10, 2018. http://www.ctheory.net/articles.aspx?id=154.

Lyotard, Jean-François. 1988. *The Differend: Phrases in Dispute.* Translated from French by Georges van dem Abbeele. Manchester: Manchester University Press.

Paić, Žarko. 2007. *Traumas of Differences.* Zagreb: Meandar.

Sutlić, Vanja. 1988. *How to Read Heidegger: Introduction to the Problematic Level of "Sein und Zeit" and Related Scriptures.* Zagreb: A. Cesarec.

Žižek, Slavoj. 2000. *The Ticklish Subject.* London: Verso.

———. 2003. *Organs Without Body: Deleuze and Consequences.* London and New York: Routledge.

5

Life as a Biopolitical Machine

5.1 Introduction

Obscenity, eroticism and pornography have passed away. What still produces the effects of pseudo-shock, provocation and embarrassing reactions of so-called social relations in the contemporary world of the perverted economy, politics and culture is more the emptiness of that world than its possibilities for the progress of outdated news. A culture that rests on the symbolic order of language as an iconoclastic sign—"You cannot become a picture, because you cross the boundaries set by the law of pleasure that is indescribable and inaccessible!"—finds self-justification in the transgression of the body itself. Where there are no more prohibitions and where everything is allowed, the final-frontier bans and admissibility do not come from below, even after a single *point* taken away in the things that equate humans, animals and machines—in absolute lust for disappearance in the clear light/nothingness. That last limit might be the final borderline between the finality and infinity of life itself.

The notion of bounds has already been understood by Hegel in his critique of bad infinity in the novel sense of the necessity of the definition

© The Author(s) 2019
Ž. Paić, *White Holes and the Visualization of the Body*,
https://doi.org/10.1007/978-3-030-14467-8_5

of every concept acquired by the construction of a subject. Without limitations in the very concept of the border, it is no longer possible to find that the current identity is anything but difference. The boundary is neither a mathematical problem nor a problem of space. This would be a problem of the openness of an event in which life in its very life (without) is bound to open and spread in such a way that it is torn apart and shared. And finally, that is a reason why we are talking about fractal and fragmented identities today.

The postmetaphysical culture of the contemporary world is quite uncannily transparent. Man and animal are equated in the anthropological desiring machine. It denotes animal life, and mentalizes humans humanely, instead of elevating to the higher degree where we cannot talk about dialectically pervading (Agamben 2004). We might add that the equalization of traditionally hierarchically distributed entities should be confirmed as well as the achievements of new scientific research. When modern biogenetics proves that the genome of the mouse is almost identical to that of a human, there is a lack only of the so-called natural dignity of man. Much more has disappeared: the metaphysical rank of the being who no longer thinks that his own is to be divine, but the openness of all beings is now seen from the openness of the life-equalling Being. However, life does not mean the openness of the original life of the self, but rather of the reproductive life technology. It is therefore obvious that what Sloterdijk and Agamben call a "human park", or the "anthropological machine", requires a different turning point in anthropology itself.

Is man still at the centre of this discourse? To this question, one of the founders of philosophical anthropology, Helmuth Plessner, responded with the assumption of man as the creature of *eccentric positionality* (Plessner 1981). "Man" can be physically open to the world in its substitute, "unnatural" positionality. So eccentricity cannot signify a decentring of a subject. Quite the contrary, it shows the displacement of the aforementioned being in its spirituality beyond the natural environment to the outside world (*Umwelt*). When the world disappears in its openness, man cannot exist in this process of the disappearing horizon of the world's worldliness somewhere in the heavenly spheres. The disappearance of man in the iconoclasm of the historical avant-garde of contemporary art was the beginning of the technology or understanding of part of a biotechnological network of structures and functions (organs without the body). The rush of modern anthropological research is to be seen primarily as an attempt to defend a new territory of man in his iconoclastic world of media eccentricity (Belting 2001).

5.2   Turn Prospects

Deleuze opened up the possibility that the world itself in his perverted social form of the schizophrenia of capitalism can be understood as the *machine*. The idea of a machine is uncanny human–inhumane. It is a condition of every remaining form of humanity and any remaining animality. The living machine represents a lively body—a picture of reality that is already virtual as such. That is a reason why culture should be not a field of value and why values can no longer be established as either God's or human. They are neither formal nor material. When Nietzsche proclaimed this period as the long period of nihilism, the first thought was of a permanent collapse of value. The value-correction request continues to manifest itself by remaining in the same circle of culture as new value. Values and culture also rely on the assumption that lifeless life is something intact, something eternal and unchangeable. But is it not that the assumption of any possible narrative of the extraversion of culture is based on erroneous and illusory premises?

Biopolitics, hence, signified the notion that Foucault introduced in contemporary thinking in the research on the notion of power from antiquity to the modern world of a ruling instinct on original human life. Due to Agamben, that term has now expanded to all areas of global capitalism analysis as a decentralized power system for which human life lies in the position of a second-rate substance. Life, therefore, precedes the political articulation of power. But in an attempt to be able to lead a life in the contemporary world, there is a turn of the metaphysical scheme. Instead of living as the openness of a Being that enables perversions of power (biopolitics), the very life of all creatures might now be generated as a biotechnological reality. However, biopolitics represents a modern articulation of life under the authority of a politically powerful machine of exclusion of all people who are not recognized as citizens of a sovereign political community.

Of course, it has always been marked by a community related to birth origin. The nation-state as a foundation of the international order of the modern age already lies in its foundations from the degeneration of what it rests on—the ideas of natural law. What if nature is nothing "natural"? Nature and life can only be called what is constructed with the subject of exclusion. So that a nation-state order could have its self-determination in the reign of the territorial sovereignty of peoples, a distinction should be made between nature (chaos) and culture (values). In this delimitation, life first appears as control over nature and culture by means of surveillance over the birth of people within the territorial boundaries of the modern nation-state. Biopolitics is, therefore, the modern control of the state, society and culture over the human body in all aspects of its life. State, society and culture are therefore not spaces of unlimited freedom of the person, but spaces of exclusion. The architectural form of absolute exclusion and control over the body is determined by the concentration camp. Here we will not deal with biopolitical analyses performed from Foucault and Agamben to Esposito, for example. The problem that lies in the theory of the contemporary turning towards the body might be leading the question of why the disappearance of the difference between man, animal and the machine itself appears as an entry in the "transcendental camp" area. That is, how does Deleuze define the meaning of biopolitics in modern times?

Under such a strange concept, there is no question of any subject or object of physical imprisonment within the institutions of modern politics. As we have already shown by the analysis of his anti-philosophy of immanence, it is a relationship to something that has the possibility, or that possibility is denied the reaction of feelings to the affirmative power of biopolitics. Bodiless bodies are, apparently, metaphorically related to the real trade in organs of global capitalism as its mode of biotechnological reproduction of life. No doubt, the key could still be something essential. The transcendental camp represents a metaphor, not a strict term. But that is the reason why it is binding. The body in its openness to the world should be no longer subject to any external label. How then could it be possible that Deleuze suggests this notion of the possibility–inability to react of the senses to something uncanny, just like affirmative biopolitics (Esposito 2008: 191–194)? It seems paradoxical to use the term that belongs to something that the body, after Deleuze and Guattari's *Anti-Oedipus* and *A Thousand Plateaus*, has nothing to do with. If the body, in its openness and eccentricity, might be immune to the definitions that historically and epochally suspended its nature in the navy of the watchdogs and the freely chosen dungeons of the postmodern permissible culture, then the term transcendental camp indeed should be the exclusion of the intention of Deleuze's entire effort to contemplate the contemporary world in the horizon of the disappearance of the body as a desiring machine. What is really going on right there? The biopolitical machine is nothing more than an anthropological or human park (Agamben–Sloterdijk), which is placed in a state of rest in a transcendental camp.

These are the social relationships of absolute control over the body that do not arise any more from the desire to destroy another (the body). On the contrary, now we should note that the turn is totally performed in all fields of life. Lacan said that the subject did not want to conquer the Other as an object by subduing its body, but by seducing its desire. Machines are a lust for what matters as a war machine, and in addition a way in which global capitalism works, primarily regarding the inner movement of its structure and other essential tendencies. It cannot rest on its starting position and wait until someone determines the final purpose. There is a paradox, but also the immanent limit of differentiating a man as an anthropological machine in a state of stillness (evolution). Who is actually there—man or machine? This must be understood as an event of completion of human evolution in the biological sense. The end of history is at the very end of bodily history as a life's progress from the simple to the complex, structurally determined, organic development of the very man in the community of other creatures (animals and plants). But the problem is that the anthropological or biopolitical machine exists in an environment where its obsolescence has already been determined. This is the environment of obsolete social relations. So the prohibition is the same as that which Marx in *Capital* placed on the sole basis of any possible social revolution of capitalism—between the prosperity/development of the forces of production (technology) and the foundations of production (society–culture). The *stability of change* (the term used by

Vanja Sutlić and Martin Heidegger) of the new world stems from the fact that its essence is already in a state of enframing (*Gestell*). Even the term anthropological machine is therefore not appropriate. The biopolitical machine might be more appropriate, because it relates to the new construction of the world (of life) as a biopolitical construction of society and culture. It can only be understood in that the "transcendental camp" does not point to any scope for changing the subject's consciousness. The body beyond the higher and lower definitions can only be truly thought of as the unity of human–animal–machine relations by generating new relationships that are "reciprocal transcendence" (Esposito 2008: 192).

It is now apparent that relations within the immaturity of the body are reciprocal relationships in the camp of transcendence. If the body no longer obeys any external determinations, either to the natural or sociocultural Father/Law, then a different kind of differential liberation of the contemporary body occurs. Surprised by matter between things in number (communication), image (visuality) and word (text), the body no longer has autonomy within itself. It is embedded in the structural zone of the struggle between technology (productive forces) and society–culture (productive relations). Productive relations, or relationships that determine society and culture as the remainder of a biopolitical machine's history at its end, derive from productive forces (technology and science). Staying in stability must be the necessity of continuous reproduction of new forms of self-production. In one of Marx's explanations from *Economic and Philosophic Manuscripts of 1844* on the question of what social relationships are, and what this man actually defines as a man in history as a way of his social existence, is said to be nothing but the primordial strength of life's power. So life is being perceived as an activity (*work, energeia, activities*; Marx and Engels 1981).

Relationships which are articulated in society, therefore, are already placed with the original strength of something that is related to the primordial power (*vis activa, potentio activa*). We could radicalize the thing and say that Marx's critique of capitalism has been a criticism of the biopolitical (re)production of social power that ends in the concept and idea of a scientific-technological "human park". The question is whether Marx was the one who believed in that old-fashioned image of man. His anthropological critique of Hegel's absolute spirit never, however, does away with the need for more awareness-raising in the scientific-technical world. The myth about the original humanity of man is already in social relations. Its traces remain in Marx's early papers. Man, though, is represented as the totality of social relations. So it is simultaneously being-there in the process of creating what becomes subject-substance. Becoming a man corresponds to the becoming of consciousness that has passed the degrees of self and selfhood. From the standpoint of Hegel's absolute spirit, man is realized in his humanity only when the unity of the idea and the concept of reality are realized. Therefore, independent anthropology without any relation to the historical movement of the idea of man within the history of the Absolute resembles the illusion of the subject—that is, the Master of history—which no longer governs because history has reached its end.

The pure immanence in the transcendental camp spoken of by Deleuze is nothing but the absolute omnipresence of life. Therefore, in this turn, the body is no longer transcendent, it is placed into the world as a new life-world of self-definition of culture as value. But let us not forget that this postulate should be more about opposing the system-world and the life-world, as Habermas put it in the traces of Husserl. All that is still maintained under these concepts becomes the only illusion and ideological sketch of a divine–human space of some pure humanity. The phrase about humanity can only have a sense of something else if it is no longer a transcendental camp for any form of inhuman being. Due to technology as a Being (enframing) of the contemporary world, it would be possible to finally put the question of the entire binary scheme of this end of history. So it is not like enframing (*Gestell*) or any form of self-determination of the human within a biopolitical machine, as the social relations of the perversion of the power of global capitalism no longer correspond to a new part of the life of the body itself. By the disappearance of the difference between bodies without organs and organs without bodies, the visual fascination of the body in the digital environment of the world as absolute constructions goes into fascination by the very act of emptying the Being and by the act of all the visual forms of the body disappearing in the nothingness of absolute light. Let us recall the end of *Season in Hell* by Arthur Rimbaud:

However, this is a dream: we take all the influences and the real gentleness. And at dawn, armed with earnest patience, we will enter in the shining cities. (Rimbaud 1976)

Entering in the "shining cities" corresponds to the visualization of the world emptied of any other determinations than those that arise from the body itself in the world. It is a visual fascination, because the image of the world itself is reduced to the biopolitical machine of life. Technology has represented the "true" Being of the contemporary world, its simulacrum that precedes all other bodies of simulations. The disappearance of the credibility of psychoanalysis as the "big narrative" of the immanence of the body-image of life occurred long before any formal *corporeal turn* occurred. In the seminal study of all the boundaries of the form of expression in the decentered world, regarding the experience of relativity in the notion of time as it is represented by Lawrence Durrell's *The Avignon Quintet*, in the final novel about the astonishing gnostic named *Quinx* with the subtitle *Ripper's Tale*, we are faced in one place with the essence of the overall *corporeal turn*. Namely, the writer says that the world has a hybrid face, made by an insect brain and constructed as a lizard. So it seems that a creature really rules the world as a beast, just like a monster without any human relics. Let us recall that reality in modern fiction is represented by a strange fictional hyper-realism or inability to reach a single certitude about what is that uncanny thing named the Real. As in Lacan's assumption that the Real exists in the imaginary and symbolic encounter in a gap faced with the real world, so in *Quinx* there is a completely distressed relationship between the so-called subject of narrative and the world of text.

The novel, in fact, begins by recalling Bruce Drexel, but soon we find out that this is a "false" recall, because he does not tell us about any realities (Durrell 1984). We suddenly comprehend that it is, actually, a novel written by Robin Sutcliff. But very soon it shows us that he is also a fictional character in a novel written by Aubrey Blanford, one of the main figures of the whole *Avignon Quintet*. They are all real and simulacra too, so their reality is not so-called objective reality, but rather one that produces reality—the fictitious reality of the novel. Thus, the body, in its disappearance in the pure visualization of the world, has become a "camp of immanence" of what is left of the spirit of its own nullity. The beast that governs the world is obviously transhuman. However, the posthuman connection between man, animal and machine gives beasts the features of something quite other than what they had in themselves: the concept of the beast in the sense of predatory cruelty to man and tough animals. Its character might be nothing monstrous. It is just an uncanny thing that in essence constructs the reality of the world itself. When the imaginary and symbolic value of writing into the body-image all possible references from the disintegrated circle of society and culture disappears, it can only then be apparent that the "lizard in the lava armour" is not a symbol or a fantasy of life as a biopolitical machine without a world. On the other side of the imaginary and the symbolic, that beast is represented by the most (hyper)realistic reality of all. That is why the real question of contemporary thinking, contemporary art and contemporary life is this: How else can we live in the age of the disappearance of Being and life itself in the technological world performed as a biopolitical machine? Does turning around the body and the absurd mean an absence of what was called the spiritual Being of man? Culture may be humanist only in terms of values that are not, but should be. This is precisely why nihilism is "living" for the duration of opposing the subject and the object. That is so confused by the use of this notion as well as the abuse of the concept of identity.

Already with Hegel and his constructive dialectics, the issue of the body has been solved. The body is, therefore, the manifest form of absolute expression in a subjective and objective spirit. Any destructive dialectics such as those of Marx, and the deconstructive view of the overcoming of the Hegel–Marx boundaries in Derrida's and Deleuze's works, were particularly an attempt to escape from the vicious cycle of overcoming and abolition (*Aufhebung*) in the sense of elevating to a higher level, ending with the idea of a social structure of man in spiritual and bodily organization. All that has happened in contemporary art and philosophy and afterwards has occurred in the direction of bodily visualization of the identity of the Being, beings and the essence of man. The problem we are faced with here might be not differences between humans and animals, because in the biopolitical (or anthropological) machine the differences between human and animal have vanished. What remains is a puzzle in the very concept itself of living, the liveliness of life on which they are built, which can all be overcome by contemporary thought and art from the 1960s to the present.

When at the very beginning of the historical avant-garde the ultimate commandment was given that life must overcome the difference between art and society, art and the world, the question of the reality of what is happening with the work of art in a "living" space and in real time has become the centre of artistic intervention. Life had the power of something uncanny. The reality of life has come from the idea that it is an inexhaustible power of disobedience to all forms of systematic discipline. We have seen Artaud's theatre of cruelty of all the notions of metaphysics, only preserving the notion of art and the livelihood of life. Is that not uncanny? Is life so powerful and resistant to all constructive-destructive techniques and sciences? Biogenetics has closed the door for us still to talk about a virgin humanism and a subject. But in the end, what kind of life is this work if not reproductive, artificial, but always constructively constructed from something that is immanent to its very life—its substitutability with a "second life"?

The image of such a "second life" is present in the body of "this" life here. Jesus Christ apocalyptically says that the Kingdom of God is already here. It is not somewhere there, but rather here and now. The other world should be a radically different other life only when this world and this life become worldly and life-open to the human possibilities of true life. Behind the emptiness, the communication, the visuality and the body, there is no socio-cultural possibility of leaving the body beyond the body itself. When we talk of life's life as such, we think of something completely different than the physiological, psychological and philosophical, as well as Jesus' image of life. We think of life as the equivalence of the Being in its event in time beyond the mere lifespan of the stability of change (the nihilism of its infinite infinitude). Truly turning is a radical thought of the pre-turn of life in the biopolitical machine of Being. It denotes a departure from the space–time of the transcendental camp (Deleuze) and entering the light of a one-off world, in its "white holes" of life without the constant desire to overcome and recover the world.

The situation in which we find ourselves only by analogy corresponds to what is called the *intermezzo of the worlds* (Vanja Sutlić). In fact, it can no longer be said that the old one has disappeared, and yet the new one is still out of sight. Old and new timelines of the past and the future are obtained from time's ecstasy of the present as actuality. When everything is only up to date, then it is all a life-long new age, a mere exploration of the "new" that cannot be preserved differently than the old-new in the eternal circle as a retro-futurism but a long-established "new" idea. What follows from such a situation? The return to the body has already happened and has played forever. As for the role of obscenity, eroticism and pornography, so can we say for the arts, religion and philosophy at the end of history. With the boredom of lifeless life, there is only a continuous *revival* of ideas that have long been lifeless since they are serious in concept and reality. What are they doing here today? With the experience that by reducing all metaphysical categories to the body in its immanence, the history of the image has been realized as a visual fascination with the body.

It would be significant to say that this is not just a problem of reviving aesthetics, the philosophy of art, the theory of art, the sociology of globalization and visual meta-theory according to the contemporary world. Moreover, the real problem we are talking about is at the very heart of what we call the horizon of the contemporary world as a set of thoughts and Being in its self-determination. Reducing the world to the life-world has already been a reduction of Husserl's thinking on the surrounding world or something called "regional ontology". In the late 1960s, the entire path of the transformation of philosophy into theory as a turning point towards *language, image, space, complexity, body* takes place as a multitude of "small narratives" about the collapse of the world's wholeness to its fragments.

5.3 Conclusion

Now we can no longer go on in the same tone of false news about the subject's renewal. The irreversibility of life creates the other side of its biopolitical substitution. Life has its meaning in the power of a singular event that is played only once as a project of its own fragile freedom. Whether this project will still be a truly artistic play in the event of real time pre-turns all these theoretical turns to *language, images, space, complexity, body* in the only lifetime of all—the openness of the event itself. Without the possibility of openness of the other and different epoch to this, which takes place in the biopolitical machine of life, there is nothing more than an unimaginable exploration of one and the same. The body is more than the captivity of soul and spirit within its own bounty. It is in its "freedom" only when the spiritual being of this body is led and directed to it in the direction of fulfilling its own life as a project in which nothing is more than human, not just in Being, but rather in the prospects of openness with which life emerges and disappears as a world. The greatest turning point in contemporary thinking as the greatest possible pre-turn should be simply that from the spiritual life of the Being, in the moments of the greatest possible threat, the Being of the very flashy openness of the "new" world. So the body has played its own game. Maybe it would be time to come to the singular contingency of the "new" world of life. The remnants of the past are redirected to the future without restriction in the very authentic sense of temporality. Looking from that perspective, which goes beyond the borders of the very core of metaphysics as the true life of the mind, searching for a simple path of thinking without any single restraint from previous thoughts is opening quite other doors on Earth as a wandering lonely star (*astēr planētēs*).

In the 458th fragment of Pessoa's *The Book of Disquietude*, written by Bernard Soares as an assistant bookkeeper in the city of Lisbon, we can read these final words:

> What I see is no longer Reality: it's just a Life.
> (…) Yes, the life to which I also belong, and which also belongs to me: and no longer Reality, which belongs only to God or to itself, which contains neither mystery nor truth, and which, because it is real or pretends to be, exists somewhere unmovingly, free of being temporal or eternal, an absolute image, as of an exteriorized soul. (Pessoa 1991: 295)

The absolute image of life goes beyond the body as its incoming pathway. This is a picture of the Absolute as an event that has happened a long time ago. But there is still only a reversal of life from the turn of the thinking of life itself; all others should be seemingly and inescapably moving around in the circle of empty signifiers.

References

Agamben, Giorgio. 2004. *The Open: Man and Animal.* Translated from Italian by Kevin Attell. Stanford, CA: Stanford University Press.

Belting, Hans. 2001. *Bild-Anthropologie: Enwurf für eine Bildwissenschaft.* Munich: W. Fink.

Durrell, Lawrence. 1984. *Quinx or Ripper's tale.* London and Boston: Faber & Faber.

Esposito, Roberto. 2008. *Bios: Biopolitics and Philosophy.* Translated from Italian by Timothy Campbell. Minneapolis and London: University of Minnesota Press.

Marx, Karl, and Friedrich Engels. 1981. *Ausgewählte Werke.* Vol I. Berlin: Dietz.

Pessoa, Fernando. 1991. *The Book of Disquietude.* Translated from Portuguese by Richard Zenith. Manchester: Carcanet.

Plessner, Helmuth. 1981. *Die Stufen des organischen und der Mensch: Einleitung in die philosophische Anthropologie.* Frankfurt/M: Suhrkamp.

Rimbaud, Arthur. 1976. *A Season in Hell.* Translated from French by Paul Schmidt. New York: Harper & Row. [Online] Accessed November 12, 2018. http://www.mag4.net/Rimbaud/poesies/Farewell.html.

6

Event and Difference: The Performative-Conceptual Turn of Contemporary Art

6.1 Introduction

In the previous chapter, I tried to show far-reaching consequences related to the problem of visualization of the body with regard to the various new phenomena of socio-cultural discourse about sexuality, technology and the desire for freedom. Thus, the biopolitical production of power can be proved by the matrix of any further theorizing of life's immediacy as such. In this chapter, I will examine how within the field of contemporary art and its events, the struggle and the confrontation between the aesthetic object and the performative-conceptual turn of the freedom of the human body take place. It will be seen, in fact, that within the aesthetic of events this radical break with the metaphysical understanding of the body encompasses the whole life-world, and how we are on the road to overcoming the contradiction between the unliving and the living, the object and the body. In the transition from "image ontology" to the "performative-conceptual turn", I will attempt to show in that way that all concepts and categories of contemporary art are more than reflections of the event in the space and time of networked virtualities. All this presupposes an insight that gives the body much more than the twisting of objects and

© The Author(s) 2019
Ž. Paić, *White Holes and the Visualization of the Body*,
https://doi.org/10.1007/978-3-030-14467-8_6

things, energy and intensity. The body embodies in its freedom of existential resistance to the world, not as a metaphysical event of a predetermined destiny. If we approach just that way to this problem, then it might be evident how in the era of the technosphere the last trace of freedom comes from the body's unwaveringness and its desire to transform into other and different forms of existence even beyond the biologically specific substance. In general, contemporary art "today" represents a paradoxical way of realizing this freedom in the world of aesthetic objects as a society of the spectacle.

6.2   Time without Words?

If we try to define a distinctive word of our own time, we will obviously find ourselves with an unexpected problem. Is there a word in spoken language as a real statement of its "age"? If it could be improved, is it possible that language might be in a condition to overcome its epochal boundaries? We are talking about our technological world using ancient languages. But the unexpected problem might be even greater if we are unable to answer the question of why "our" age should ever have its own language if we are not sure that we are acclimatized to the atmosphere right there, but, on the contrary, we feel like strangers in it, as Hölderlin predicted in elegies for the mythical world of the ancient Greeks. To have our "own" time does not mean to be governed by it. Joining it means to be with it in confidence, and also close to the distances from it. If this should be the "age" of a certain something that transcends trust and closeness, then it is uncanny in its power of destruction of the work of any attempt to leave it in the presence of trace material. Moreover, the language of our "time" has become a mere technical means of communication, tools, apparatus, machine. In that, we could detect the real problem. Hence, when language becomes a physical machine to write the subject as an actor in the historical drama of identity, it should be performed on itself and thereby change the perception, and then nothing is more certain and self-explanatory in the entire world. So the destruction of language obviously represents a reliable sign of the loss of worldliness of the world itself. Undoubtedly, "our" age is determined by the technical reproduction of the body. It occurs at the same time and disappears at the time of unrepeatable singularity. As an event-specific difference between "living" and "artificial", "life" and "art", the body is transformed into a multitude of figures and forms. This age is the age of the performative-conceptual turn of the body. Meaning, thus, denotes a reversal in the aesthetic configuration of science and technology which constructs reality. All that takes time encompasses the presence of features ("now"), instantaneous and virtual. That is a reason why "our" era belongs to "us" and "them". Simply, the desire and demand for some other time "when wishing still helped", as Peter Handke said in his book *Live without Poetry*, encompass the universe of things related to our joyful thinking as an existential adventure. When there is no more beautiful and sublime, from the production of an event arises a need for the aesthetic design of the surrounding world. But the claim to transcend his own time as a terrifying experience of the freedom of the contemporary man might also be denoted as a need for genuine freedom of life itself, no matter whether it is genuine or something mythical or utopian and vanishing. Therefore, we could describe that as a necessarily emergent aesthetics of the event. It connects all the previously separate forms of contemporary art such as installations, actions, happenings, conceptuality and contextuality. Performative art should be the last possibility of saving life, liberty and living embodiment. The essence of human uniqueness and singularity is shown here in the presence of coherent bodies. When everything becomes reproductive and batched, bare and vital life confronts the reality of things. Can this possibility, despite the apparent overproduction of performance and performativity today, be truly subversive and lead to radical changes in the world of the "spirit" of contemporary art, or just sheer aesthetics in a variety of other aesthetics, for example illusion, perception, atmosphere, digitality? What is performative art in general, if the body creates the real ground of life, its freedom according to the assumption of unassailability?

> Performance art is art without works. It happens in the midst of "art". It creates in the one single act, in the immediate gesture, singular action, in the event. It takes self-reflection of the avant-garde, the art system as meta-art. In its place comes an open process, project, time... (...) Art becomes a

feast of pure emptiness and fullness. So, it appears as a sovereign of Nothingness; her métier becomes an evocation of "effectiveness". (Mersch 2002: 245)

To be active and effective means nothing else than to be-in-the-act, to be in the action in the way Aristotle understood movements—*dynamis* and *energeia*. Performative art might be the primarily ecstatic activity of the body in the transgression of its borders. That borders were given by the establishment of modern politics and culture as an ideology (Paić 2005). Of course, bodies in the performance of their liberty are facing the ideological-political boundaries of the modern era. Instead of the tragic fate of the Greek notion that Nietzsche reformulated as *amor fati*, and then the modern obsession with the representation of the world on the stage as a reflexive activity of the subject and its autonomy, the contemporary era has provided temporary and changing situations and contexts. Freedom is quite embodied in them. The term which I used right there implies a situation already existent in social relations—an entity acting in its own performance as an actor in existence with others—while the notion of context should be understood as a diagram of culture with its writing of differences (language–speech–body). Therefore, the body is always a contextual encounter with the Other in the contingency of situations—the main feature of the situation we define as a temporary event. The effectiveness of freedom as the feast of the game with "emptiness" and "fulfilment"—from Dadaist provocation and shock—determines the experimental stations of the world as an assemblage of language–speech–body. That is a fundamental problem with the definition of performative art in what it is doing and acting. If performative art did "something" now, or if the event might be "not" because it is the work of a being or an object, it would be obvious that the keyword of contemporary philosophy and art in the direction of overcoming being has become the keywords and concepts of contemporary philosophy and art, as well as the representation and symbolic signifying of the world. Between modernity and the contemporary age there exists a feedback relationship. Modernity was from the very beginning based on the cult of making new ones. But it goes beyond that, because every type of modern awareness means a loss of orientation in the "present". That could be the reason why contemporary art in its immersion in this "now" performatively embodies/incarnates the mystery of the moment as a flash of eternity. The true beginning was an aim of Cézanne's entire process of painting: it was still in that moment that he reached the fullness of the painter and the emptiness of the world. Therefore, Dadaism in advance has explicitly drawn attention to the a-logical (language), aleatory (speech) and performative (the body). At the time of the historical avant-garde in the 1920s, art tended to the self-realization of man as the idea of living in the new society created with modern industry. Paradoxically, the historical mission of the avant-garde was that it simultaneously opened the door to the unfinished progress of science and technology and celebrated the primordial chaos of life. In Berlin, Dada in action was the linguistic and musical art of turning images into an event of physical self-presence (Hans Richter, Hans Arp, Hugo Ball). It seems reasonable, without causing overt actions, to reverse the rank of discursive power. Language is established as the alienated and reified apparatus of the metaphysics of history by the contemporary age in the form of metalinguistic "nature", or in the form of natural language "stuff". In Western history, language has developed into the complex structure of amputation or castration of unconscious desires in the name of the sublime object of things. When a language no longer is spoken in its uncanny depths of traumatic history, it remains only to communicate on the market as the exchange of information activities.

Thus, the criticism of language's critique of metaphysics means a-logical and aleatoric techniques to reverse the binary opposition of nature–culture, and their abolition in the non-identical Third. When a new Dada artist protests against the legalized system of the rule of language in the form of the natural Father/Law, then the function of manifestation in the avant-garde is represented as a cognitive-critical mapping of intermediality in the performative-conceptual turn of contemporary art. Dieter Mersch, in his interpretation of the relationship between language and contemporary art, said that the problem is that the structure of art direction goes beyond the notion of representation of word-picture. A physical manifestation of the event is thus losing the privileged place of meaningful narratives. The materiality of speech in historical avant-garde art—from the novel *Berlin Alexanderplatz* by Alfred Döblin to poetry, and the edges of the fracture between Being and Nothingness in the poetry of Paul Celan and the experimental music of John Cage—might be placed in the centre of the performative-conceptual turn. Insanity, infantilism, primitivism, silence, emptiness, nothing—these are all hieratical masks of the totally reverse world. Symbolic speech in such a world displays or represents nothing more. Two terms, hence, are arising from the aesthetics: the *objet trouvé* of Kurt Schwitters and Marcel Duchamp's *readymades*. Both findings were preexisting in the reality of the modern industrial era and society appropriating this age of science and technology. Things already found in the reality of an industrial society are identical to the ready-to-use. So the pragmatic essence of language corresponds to the status of the instrumental body language as an object/thing. Dadaism in its most radical form of Schwitters and Duchamp appears as the performative realization of ideas, and finally as the conceptual turn of contemporary art. This event denotes a realization of freedom and the difference between the living world (body) and systematic control of the world (apparatus and *dispositif*). The objects replace the subjects. Instead of raising the autonomy of action, it takes place as a play of differences between language and speech (the body) in a social situation and cultural context (Mersch 2002; Paić 2006). Thus, the replacement might be the process of production to the limit of the aestheticized performative object. So the aesthetic object is represented as a "still-life body", but only a living body in its performativity can be a true model according to the projection of the object as an entity of fulfilled wishes. Without the desire to possess things and their transformation into objects, it would be truly impossible to perform any kind of political economy of capitalism. Therefore, the digital delirium of aestheticizing capitalism represents simply the last stage of the disappearing of the difference between life and art (technosphere and biosphere).

If we try to establish an approach to the problem in that way of thinking, then we are faced with a turn in the structure of metaphysics in general. Namely, instead of speaking about the history of symbolic language (art) in all its forms and ways of expressing presentation—literature, painting, sculpture, architecture, dance, music, theatre—the very physicality of a life of freedom requires a revolution in language. This is a reversal of the previous condition of possibility in the world. What some philosophers like Rorty called the notion of the "linguistic turn" or

Habermas' notion of "postmetaphysical thinking" (*nachmetaphysisches Denken*) is nothing but trouble coming up with the contingency and openness of the body in its relation to Being and Nothing. In other words, the body regains its dignity of speech only when the language of metaphysics collapses in the debris. It continues to follow the universal character of visuality. And that no longer points to anything other than other characters or other bodies as objects in space and time. Baudrillard proclaimed, from that point of view, the end of semiotics and determined the actual performance of "integral reality" which is established in biotechnically managed code (Baudrillard 1998). The death of the language of metaphysics, therefore, is the beginning of body language as postmetaphysical events beyond the "point", "meaning" and "referentiality", beyond the representation of reality, beyond the binary opposition between "nature" and "culture". The shocking naked body on the scene/stage of the experiment and its transformation into a technical exhibition organized within the machine system of production–consumption link two apparently radically opposed approaches to the "world": one determines the life of the body as a non-subjugated existence of freedom, while the other is reflected in the artificial nature of the aesthetic or industrial buildings of civilization.

Duchamp's case in contemporary art is paradigmatic for understanding the scope of the performative-conceptual turn. His idea to delineate the entire aporia aesthetic event and all the problems with non-working, artistic (re)action changes the world into language–speech–body situations and the contexts of modern and postmodern society. Since this is a radical step into the very life out of art which cannot be done without a radical change in art, and it is not just an illusion of beauty and sublimity in Kant's sense of purposefulness without purpose and disinterested pleasure, it should be clear that art has to take on the meta-artistic mission to promote the ideas of radical change in the world. We must keep in mind that it seems to be obvious that the avant-garde does not have its own aesthetic. Instead, it has no foundation in the autonomy of art, but rather in the ethical act of ideological-political change of life itself. That is a reason why from Dadaism and the related historical avant-garde movement of the first half of the twentieth century, we are still talking about the totality of life. Consequently, it manifests itself in the event and its difference in reflexive consciousness. The performative art scandal, which runs on a shocking scene, without meaning to life itself as a chaotic magma being in all its excremental secretions, derived from the contingency of Being. Indeed, the case shows the materiality of reality without the requirement of virtual possibilities that are absolutely other and different. When Croatian neo-avant-garde artist Željko Jerman in his conceptual act of rebellion against "this" world "here" and "now" expressed the irrefutable credo of all subversive movements of the artistic avant-garde—*This is not my world*—then we are immersed in the scopes of art and life without foundation. The scandal does not include nudity and obscenity on the scene/stage, where one can urinate and rave, make a grimace face to face of Other as a witness and participant of "this" and not the "other" (the world). The scandal, instead, designates a conflict between the freedom of the living body and its (necessary and inevitable) death in the reproductive event of repetition. Freedom is dying in the living body part as an aesthetic object. This might be the most scandalous case of the ever-banal tragic fate of the performative-conceptual turn of contemporary art. There are no events without distinction as reproductions of life. To be played as a live art performance requires a third party. This could be nothing more than what the Greeks, namely Plato, called by the word *techné* and attributed to art as a production (*poiesis*) designating an uncanny assemblage. The new comes into the world first and foremost thanks to the concept of *techné* known from ancient Greek metaphysics (Agamben 1999).

6.3   The Meaning of Duchamp's Transformations

In the book that emerged from a panel discussion at the colloquium on "Performance in Postmodern Culture" at the University of Milwaukee in 1976, philosopher Jean-François Lyotard at the beginning says that like many others he has difficulties with understanding the word "performer". Therefore, he proposes to replace this word with something more understandable—*transformer* (Lyotard 1990: 31). He found the reasons in

Duchamp's work of 1914 on fabrication entitled *Standard Stoppages*. There is, namely, the emergence of a new figure thanks to the effects of photographic projections: apparatus figures derived from the transformation of cinematic energy. In its motion, light visualizes the figure in terms of completely changing the viewer's identity. If there is no apparatus, therefore, there is no possibility of changing the life-world and art. "Apparatus" should be considered ambiguous: (1) as a set of technical conditions that produce a new image object and the object (analogue and digital photography); and (2) as a life-existential complex of diverse activities that advance the action, constituting historical discourse in the form of body language and performative practices. This notion is another name for Foucault's *dispositif*. So the biopolitical mode of life in modern contemporary society of the control and neoliberal capitalism is a dispositive power of ideological work, and not merely a reflexive awareness of actions. Life itself in the form of action takes place as an unassailable freedom of the body and as an ideological apparatus. The secret reveals the ideology of language–speech–body in the daily performance of entities/actors in a class-divided society. So the secret takes the form of a "false consciousness" in the modern capitalist state apparatus, as follows from Althusser's supplement known by the classical Marxist theory of ideology (Žižek 1994). The apparatus is, however, the system of relations established within the whole of society, politics and culture (Foucault 1980: 2; Agamben 2009). If there are more opportunities for the transformation of matter and form, it is a more radical change. In both words, performance and transformation, there is already a pre-design, a making, the emergence of something different and other. Performance (*performare*) as pro-execution (*productio*, *poiesis*) is etymologically distinct from setting or placement (*representatio*), although each performance indicates the setting of re-presented and presented as the basis of performance (*subjectum* and *substantia*). From the period of the early modern age, it is essential to understand the changes being derived as a man comprehends the subject of re-presenting Being as a whole. The image of the world is related to the result of the early modern era. In general, the image might be determined to change the world of human thought and action (Heidegger 2003a: 75–114).

In an attempt to change some things that happened in the performance of body double (semiotic and somatic), it is necessary that only a single body in its entirety in the coming time can open the perspective (future) in this "now" and "here". Acting in the present moment that determines the performativity of the body in space presupposes something out of that terms. This point of view and the ecstatic language in the performativity of the body as a work of art itself are in the projection of the event. Without screening, the event remains essentially unrepresented, un-reproductive and un-distinctive. The basic setting designates a deconstruction of the appendix or supplements. The dissemination of traces corresponds to the polysemy of signs. No substitution or addition of a trace of the representativeness of the text is a necessary event in the disappearance of the black hole of the eternal past. Paradoxically, precisely because the action is still active in the present, it could be possible that the language has a performative character changed from the present time to the ecstasy of coming. This point is the performative character of prophetic speech. Not by chance, all the art of avant-garde manifestos is beyond discursivity. They reflect the combination of the Messianic language of revelation in the future and the performative discourse of radical changes in the present situation by all means. The meta-discursivity of a manifesto requires vigorous action (Puchner 2006).

Only work through the language–speech–body translates into action constantly moving across the boundary between life and art. That is why contemporary art is a universal code of practice in transgression of society, politics and ideology. The event lies in its projection; it reproduces and varies as a singular event from other events as time passes in a single form and a single work. Instead of being fixed, works of originality decide on singular events and the uniqueness of the case as art and freedom. The paradox might be that the very essence of the play as repetition and duplication of the original concept creates a new original work. It is authentic in its repeatability because the event produces the original time of the art-work. Authors, therefore, bestow performative action on the subject/actor. The difference lies between reproduction, replication and cloning. But the difference also lies in the notion of language, speech and body. Language is, thus, a technically reproducing apparatus or a *dispositif* of the power of social and cultural communication. Speech causes a replica in the process of communication that relies on information exchange in the performance of dialogue and discourse (Kittler 2002). Of course, the body doubles as technological transformation in the different body of the Other (*plastic surgery*). But now the work has the feature of the aesthetic object (*readymade*). When the body is transformed into something ready-made, it loses to any further way of distinguishing authentic and inauthentic, the primaeval and the secondary. In contemporary philosophy, which examines the relationship between Being and the writing of difference, Derrida shows that a concept of *différance* opens the notion of events and differences in the condition of possibility of the first and second differences, and primaeval iterability, letters and text. The performativity of language is always already inside track, playback and font relating to other clues as to other texts, archives, media (Paić 2011: 317–366).

Projections, moreover, indicate a snatching of the essential features of freedom and the future perspective of image brightness. Freedom bestows the body's aura, its light of Being. Without such a performative art, it would be a vain effort to retrieve the moon, to use Lafcadio Hearn's metaphor of the meeting of Westerners and Japanese. Each event could be already in its original events presented as a difference between two worlds that might still carry on in advance. It can almost be said that there are two events in their perfect simultaneity. The former happens effectively, while the latter concerns the events in the aspects of the work. In addition, the former is the original track and the latter encompasses the reproductive trace of artistic differences. Duchamp in his "deeds" and "events" opened a fundamental problem of contemporary art. What is art if art participates in life, but always has something much more artificial other than life itself? If, therefore, in between the two worlds has to be in between the one-off and unrepeatable event in the life of man as a physical presence *and* performance differences resulting from the transformation of bodies into human reproductive circuits working like a *transformer*, then the real discomfort of contemporary art derives from the fact that it lives in the abyss of different worlds. There is no heaven or earth, but always somewhere "in between" that requires consideration. As a matter of fact, the difference between the events of the living and the lifeless bodies of the aesthetic object have a real possibility of answering the question of why all of contemporary art since the radical faction in Berlin's Dadaism in the 1920s to the present day has been immersed in the mystique of action as the politicization of the world and the politicization of action as the mystique of the world.[1] We will discuss this topic much more at the end of this chapter. The only hint is that the concept of the *re-politicization of art* from the 1990s to the present condition is represented by the imperative of "ethical aesthetics" as a reversal of action beyond the boundaries of society, politics and ideology. Without any restraints, the body in its performative-conceptual turn causes reactions in the public space regarding the surveillance apparatus of power. *Re-enactment* determined in performances by Marina Abramović, for example, shows that forgetting the past is necessarily manifested in the form of the physical expression of social amnesia, which operates traumatically to the participants of the new events (Massumi 2011).

We would not forget the traumatic experience of a loss of historical consciousness, but the traumatic event of the return of memories in the form of necessary oblivion. Remembering the forgotten traces of events that could be rebuilt in a different situation and context as an attempt at overcoming the primal trauma should be one obvious solution. This is undoubtedly clear regarding the collective trauma of history as the radical evil of the Nazi Holocaust against the Jews in World War II. But it also applies to crimes committed during the reign of the ideology of Communism in the postwar age. The condition of memory as opposed to the self-reflective process of remembering (the apparatus of memories as such) is completely unaware of the process of development of matter and form. In the state of entropy, the flood of images and the emotions that accompany them open the remembering trace of the problem in the temporality of events. Memory, on the contrary, is represented as a conscious reproduction of the event as the upcoming assemblage of interactions and interconnectedness. Language certainly allows all memory traces to be inscribed in the singularity of the event. Therefore, memory could be always a visual effect without cause and purpose. That is what happens as the openness of the cognitive and emotional picture, features we have in the movies of Andrei Tarkovsky and Lars von Trier. In accordance with Lacan's fundamental assumption that the unconscious is articulated as language, memory, hence, assumes the discursive order of language, memory and the visual chaos of events in the physicality of life.

So the problem of remembering represents the question of performative art according to body trauma in a state of shock caused by violent society, politics and ideology, and the problem of memory is the issue of the black hole in research in archives' and museums' interpretation of history. The memory holds an unconscious language of dreams and remembering the control apparatus of social power in a strictly structured ideological-political reality. An example might be shown in the conceptual performance of transmedial Croatian artist Dalibor Martinis from the assemblage of video works entitled *Data Recovery* (Beroš 2006). The relationship between memory and remembering in the contemporary culture of musealizing and historicizing history is obviously the relationship between selective memory and chaotic remembering. In the literature, this is quite evident concerning Proust, when memory bestows a cognitive map of grooves and notches in the past (Deleuze 1964). The unconscious (picture) might be expressed as consciousness (language) on the fractures in the real trauma. Deleuze has attempted to solve this problem by introducing the term "immanence of consciousness". This stems from events like the prospects of repetition and difference. The film therefore in visual culture emerges as a modern secular worldview and religion, and not as an aesthetic model of consciousness. However, it occurs in the form of cinematic processes unfolding in movement-image and time-image. The time-image produced the dynamism of action and movement stopped during the time-image as a virtual projection of actuality which is believed to be the true picture of reality. All other images, according to this figure, are only just simulacra of reality and illusion.

When we have today changing aesthetic understanding by returning the dignity of an artistic observer of events in the figure "emancipated spectator", then it is primarily emphasis on the emancipation from the tyranny of the subject property (Lacoue-Labarthe 1998). Already Paul Klee opened the possibility of a "rebellion of objects" facing the subject, and Lacan in his theory of images referred to the triumph of the spectacle in which the object of desire marks the end of the dialectic of desire, and moves into the void of any other definition except the desire to give-to-see the Other as an object. The question of the abolition of representative works might not be dismissed merely by replacing the body with the performative act. No doubt, this act no longer needs the concept of understanding and sense of speech in the language of metaphysics, but rather uses a system of physical signs of the pragmatic speech code. In the speech of the "two worlds" and the two bodies—the events of life and differences of art; the body only as a set of existential actions and through the body as an aesthetic object that is going to be a line in between language, culture and life in general theatricalizing—arises the missing link of the modern representation and performativity of language–speech–body.

The overall critique of representation in contemporary art rests on a kind of dogma of "lifelessness" of another event or difference as repetition and reproduction (Groys 2003: 34). Since Benjamin, the issue of the technical reproduction of art has been placed at the centre not only of philosophical debate. If the technical apparatus, such as the film camera, is a condition able to transfer the work in the event of live pictures, authenticity or a single artistic aura of creativity, then it requires a different notion of the relationship between originals and copies. Of course, the turn in the contemporary media of art is that now the "aura" does not lie in the original, but rather in the spirit of technological reproduction. The same applies to the bodily presence of living performance in the scene. In fact, the body no longer recognizes the voice of metaphysical theatre, but the unpredictability and spontaneity of the body in its work on the other. The problem is in using the word "performer", as it apparently claims Lyotard, derive from that the body as machine denotes a construction/deconstruction of events seen from the viewpoint of the language, culture and medial determination of corporeality. The body should be, thus, pragmatically open like parts. As Lyotard argues, the projection produces a change of the object. The projection, in the end, is running *transformations* (Lyotard 1990: 31).

In the case of Marcel Duchamp's performance that transforms the projection of a mechanical camera into a woman, Miss Rrose Sélavy is not at all just about the physical transformation of a singular event. Right there we are faced with the simultaneous action of "two worlds". The separation of the whole life-world and the art-world is the result of the modern articulation of science, technology and society. Life and art are separated in modern society due to the fragmentation of labour and production. The totality of life is disintegrating into various sectors of activity or environment. It connects them to the necessity of exchange and communication. From Marx to Debord and further, analysis of the fragmentation of life in the system of labour and production lines has always been of the destructive dialectic of history. The apparent autonomy of both science and logic disappears in the modern technology of industrial production. The autonomy of modern art in a paradoxical way, thus, is trying to be defended in the new digital environment of contemporary capitalism, in the spaces of new media. But now, instead of the illusion of freedom of fragmentary works, we are faced with the illusion of total freedom of the artist and the audience in creating interactive and artistic events. Of course, this is not, however, the problem of autonomous acts or events. The problem lies in the destruction of the body and acts as an oversight of body/reproductive events in the presence and synthesis of living differences superseding the world as an aesthetic object in the universal screening of radical transformation. Freedom as the body controls the action of universal techno-code and denotes quite another contingency. As a matter of fact, the violence against the body in the permissive and narcissistic culture of global capitalism becomes spectacular because of its technical reproduction process, and the massacre in the contemporary world becomes quite an uncanny thing of the machine-without-desire, where we have only bodies as corpses, in the strictly materialistic manner of representation (Guattari 2009: 207–214). As the images in the digital culture of technically produced images are beyond mimesis and representation, because nothing mimics anything and does not represent anything, so only the body could be part of an assemblage in which the body language and visual projection might be a code of the contemporary *technosphere*. The problem of what is dismissed by the art world in the new situation could be solved very pragmatically. And that means by using pragmatic logic, as it assumes the institutional foundation. No more is there any kind of metaphysics which pretends to be a final answer to the question of technogenesis at all. We have quite other problems than our ancestors according to a unique way of thinking related to what is going on in the space–time of the indefinite and complexity (Paić 2011).

The body, thus, becomes an aesthetic object (readymade) when it equates its "usable" value in the market as a commodity with the exchangeable value of another body. It is not difficult to conclude that this is a perversity of modern capitalist production. Commodity fetishism as a visual representation of the secret of the society of the spectacle lies precisely in the reversal of the exchange in instrumental value or the transformation of objects (things) into the aesthetic object (capital). Visualization of the body in the new mode of production changes the cinematic energy of the contemporary world in the information economy. It is based on the interactive user who appears in the role of the recipient of visual information (Beller 2006). From the pragmatic logic in which everything is becoming an aesthetic object because of the data for communication with others inevitably follows that every possible body in the virtual space of real–performative becomes a *body-for-use*. Freedom and the case of the living body confront the necessity of reproduction and the aesthetic object. The paradox is that the latter denotes a condition of possibility of the former. Or, in other words, expressed in contemporary capitalism, commodities as an aesthetic object provide the illusion of freedom of choice between having and being. As for any possible staging of the living body, during the bio-cybernetic condition setup options mediate certain technological methods of forming the body itself, so the same happens in real life. Creating the cyborg-made body, the preservation of the living body in its transition to another form of bio-technosphere becomes the most important thing in current digital culture. This should be the case with Stelarc's *Locomotor* performance and a range of series called *Suspensions*. Speculative pragmatism at work moves in that way an opening time of an unexplored area of relations between the experience of playing the events and the experiences of their interpretation (Massumi 2002: 89–132).

The turn was uncanny and therefore has the power to legalize a fundamental contemporary perversion: something that becomes an art object is not directly a product of artistic activity, and someone who becomes an artist does not directly have the "nature" or the aura of his genius, but by setting the context of "culture" as a science and technology complex. Instead of essentialism concerning the classical definition of art as a sensible display and performance of metaphysical ideas in their glory, there is a purely *pragmatic turn*. The situation and context of art bestow artistic features, and life itself should be seen as an existential event and the action of freedom within certain situations and contexts. The dialectics is a dialectics of two worlds of non-identical synthesis. For Adorno, this has already meant the impossibility of the reconciliation of life and art of the aesthetic act of producing reality (Adorno 1973). One is determined by transforming the world of artistic works in the event of the physical presence of the subject/actor live itself as a staging area in the public gaze, and the second by transforming objects using the aesthetic object with the addition of symbolic value—two worlds acting simultaneously as two bodies with their own distinctive logic.

The first one belongs to the triad of concepts *performances, performative, performance*, and the second one to *conceptuality, conceptual, concept*. Two bodies of contemporary art from Duchamp to Stelarc thus differ due to the singular event of the vitality of life itself, like un-representable stage plays, and the difference in the reproductive repetition of such events signified the presence in the form of the aesthetic object. Regardless of whether the concept of *readymades* denotes a real or virtual materialization thereof in digital networks, new media, the same might be represented as the logic of distinction. Between the body as a living presence in performance on the stage and an aesthetic object placed in the outside world thanks to the design of industrial production, apparently there is still a difference. But is this really the case? Or perhaps we have a big deal with the necessary illusion of truth that lies behind the form of two worlds? The answer to this question is not only the answer to the question about the essence of contemporary art in general, but the answer to the question about its future and the "sense" that the world rests on the logic of the technosphere. To be able to move on, and not always to open old wine in new bottles, it seems necessary to begin to explain why we can no longer continue to talk about performance as singular and unrepeatable, and event staging and artistic life in the "moment", but it becomes necessary to take one step back and complete the performative turn in contemporary art to understand the concept of transformation as the body itself and its freedom of action. This simply means starting from the concept derived from Lyotard's interpretation of Duchamp's transformation in the projection of the body. A necessary condition for doing so lies in the performativity of language and the pragmatics of speech as a socio-cultural discourse that can play in a total time of the reign of techno-science, information policy and media culture (Lyotard 1988). The first assumption is that the performative-conceptual turn in contemporary art is happening simultaneously on three mutually interconnected levels:

1. The historical and epochal level of the performativity of language in its effective event of structural differences.
2. The structural-genealogical level of the performativity of speech incarnate as a symbolic code of other and different cultures.
3. The level of the aesthetic and theatrical staging of the body in the singularity of space and time in the media-constructed world.

Language belongs to the universal human discursive activity of speech, hence to the determination of particular cultural practices in the construction of identities; and the body in its theatrical staging of the openness of the world as a self-difference in the event produces a new situation. More precisely, language allows us to change the situation and context of action in society because language shows the truth of Being. Language is spoken. As its governor, a man could be an embodied subject/actor speaking through his own world. Wittgenstein once said that the limits of my language are the limits of my world. Without speech and language, there should be no possibility that the body in its singularity can set on the stage its own concept of performativity as the only real issue of contemporary art. And it is no longer a question of where and why (the purpose and meaning of language and speech performance), but how it would be possible that something does happen, and whether it is going to decide the features of contemporary art: a *quod* or so-being event deciding on a *quid* or what-ness (Being, substance; Mersch 2002: 245–246). Instead of metaphysical questions about the meaning of narratives, the only question now becomes a postmetaphysical question about the limits of a body shown as a picture in an unrepresentative manner. This threefold scheme seeks to implement quite a significant distinction between the two worlds and two bodies of performative art (Paić 2006: 215–281).

However, unlike the *performative turn* of contemporary art, which primarily in their studies and analyses contemporary German philosopher Dieter Mersch and theatre theoretician Erika Fischer-Lichte (Fischer-Lichte 2004) performed, I would like to elaborate the thesis represented by establishing that on the traces of Dadaism and Duchamp the technical transformation of the body (the media) could be the screening of a *performative-conceptual turn*. Each action is, thus, determined by the performative transformation of the subject/actor, the Other and the surrounding world. So, just in time for digital media, we have to talk about synthetic action to overcome the so-called autonomy of the dual spheres of contemporary art. Conceptual art as an art of the idea of activity in the world belongs in its essential intention to performative events. The reason occurs from the concept of something always acting in the public arena or the living world (Alberro 2003). This is not a mere *addition* to the vibrant presence of the body as a subject/actor living art event on the scene. Nothing there is compensated for or externally added. Mediality as the living presence of the event in its performative event will be an open operation. Therefore, the work denotes the conceptual design of the body in total transformation. As an example, we must keep in mind a queer travesty on stage or an event of the obsessive game by Jan Fabre with the transformation of the human–insect simultaneity of the events underlying the emergence of childbearing, essentially the difference between language–speech–body like the image created by media projection. This significantly changes the singularity of the event:

> *Performer (?)* is a complex *transformer*, battery machines transformation. This is not about art, because there is no object, there is only transformation, redistribution of energy. The world is a multiplicity of interconnected devices that transform the units of energy into one another. Duchamp the transformer does not want to repeat the same effects. This is why he must be many of these apparatuses and must metamorphose himself continually. (Lyotard 1990: 36)

Two assumptions should be noted:

1. There is no art without objects.
2. The world is a multiplicity of apparatuses mutually transforming the power of unity.

Lyotard's analysis is represented as an extremely important step beyond the still metaphysical framework of the notion that art issues. The framework works and reverses the relationship between signifier and signified. Objects as objects ready for use caused through industrial production (readymades) take on the character of aesthetic objects. This is because through their appearance (form and content) occurs the unfolding drama of two bodies of contemporary art: performative and conceptual. If the object of transformation might be the effect of the technosphere, then the activity of transforming the body in continuity arises as a result made by the biosphere. Separation is, thus, the illusion of having a sphere of autonomy of art as a living practice. The complex structure of the transformation involves the performance of the body in constant metamorphosis. It might be therefore already evident that the transformation event as a redistribution of energy assumes the effect of the appliance and its projections. These uncanny transformation of things due to what it does will be in between these two worlds/two bodies of contemporary art and lead to the abolition of art as an actual practice. The idea of overcoming radical art is particularly marked by Guy Debord's situationist movement in the 1950s–1960s. Its devotion to film was an obsession in the genuine character of radical conceptual act. This is a pictorial realization of the pure cinematic energy of life. Beyond the division of work and everyday life in a false synthesis of spectacular visualization of global capitalism an integrated process of the enchantment of observers' attention takes place. That is one reason why film is more than the mystery of life events, a replay of difference and the arts. Its reproductive power of the open image stems from the fact that time is the idea of film as the conceptual performative event itself. Who in the movie is a subject/actor and who is a participant; who is, in addition, an artist and who is the audience? Film as the event of the reproductive differences of life and art can only be the worklessness of events in motion. Not accidentally, Dziga Vertov himself put cinematic production—camera film—at the very heart of the event. It generates the event and produces the media reproduction of reality, and real people and their destinies are not transferred from the life of the film.

The work of art that ensures the final result of the work process in four metaphysical causes as understood by Aristotle (*causa formalis, causa materialis, causa efficiens, causa finalis*) shows that art is understood only in the procession of final acts as subject or object when it comes to architecture and the visual arts. Materiality and form are part of its predisposing structural arrangement and the spatial relationships to the temporal sequence of causes and effects. This conception of art as a result of a work of art derives from the traditional metaphysical scheme of early modern science, with its key concepts of causality, interactivity, purposefulness. It is known as a teleological model of action. Even before the real work of art occurs, what has already been completed is its idea of a purposeful process circuit of intuition and rationality. When Lyotard comes down firmly on art objects, he keeps in mind a model of organization of physical objects in order to make meaningful the historical bonds of the original and the semblance in the conceptual code of an early modern age. In it, the body must make the work within the object as a system of signs. But the body in the procession is a continuous process of transformation of identity. It establishes a body in motion without purpose in the entropy model, which goes beyond the metaphysical framework of the notion of the fact that its stability in space and time is required by the projection of transformation outside of itself. Being outside means to have the availability of an ecstatic body of the performative-conceptual turn of events in the art of life itself as a performance transformation. In this way one should understand Duchamp's radical turn: no more drawing pictures and no real art objects as aesthetic objects, because it is already a work of industrial production of the world as aesthetic objects of the world. Communication between objects (of art) becomes the interaction between the bodies (of life). Devices or tools that communicate with each other create the intermediate circuit, with no signs of its signifier and signified. It is the only single movement in the transformation. It could be noted that machines transform energy into staging different/other modes of action of the body in the event of reproductive differences. In the process of delivery of an energy event in advance, there is something uncannily inhuman as such. What exactly? It is about provocation, the being of the virtual features according to the uncanny technosphere. In addition, it works perfectly by using the principles of pragmatic-use items, and the language of the display transforms their performing possibilities into a technical circuit. From that viewpoint, the transformation of the body helped the projection energy apparatus to allow the transformation of the living body in the artistic event of the emergence of objects which are placed in the scape of absolute virtuality. That is the way we should strictly follow in advance regarding the assemblage of life, art and the technosphere (Virilio 1991).

In other words, the performative language, speech and performance of the body are possible only as a singularity of events due to projection. The body looks at the transformation—as indicated by Duchamp's transformation into a female figure—set in space as a conceptual language of images, pictures and voice of the conceptuality of concept in the bodily image that remains. The picture above cannot signify the ontological language, speech and body. Without images and a visualization of the complex postmetaphysical thinking which in its immanence is being replaced, the human being will not be a possible creation of the world from the logic of techno-scientific development.

On the question of how to preserve the work in the presence of a trace event, or other words which belong to Boris Groys, in an attempt to document contemporary art, the answer should be in advancing the implosion of information as a precondition of the media revolution of the world. Extremely radically and extremely concisely said: the idea of the museum of contemporary art as a hybrid machine of visuality, textuality, theatre and music does not exist in any monumental building of architectural work. This museum is doing an experiment and is structured within the very field of the aesthetic configuration of artificial intelligence. Or, simply, a museum of contemporary art as an idea is equivalent to the idea of biologically obsolete man—life crypt and cemetery art, to paraphrase Nietzsche. The memory card is represented as the only intelligent machine that still should have the ability to rescue virtual discursive/iconic distinctions between events and difference (reality and hyper-reality). Virtual museums are consequently a spot-free setup with no spaces or temporality. Their only justification is to represent a timelessness in a time of social networks whose functions are replacing archive files as a giddy past that might be infinitely far away from the present time which it seeks to revive. The ghostly power of the past is constantly working underground. When we are not staged, the past flows into the living openness of history. If we are staged in history, then post-totalitarian aesthetic kitsch occurs. Debord's spectacle at the concentration stage of flows, diffuse and integrated spectacle manifests the monstrous proportions of the aestheticization of the world as orgies of state/society in the global age. But the event cannot be preserved in its one-off act in any other way than as simultaneous media projection. The simultaneity of events and their artistic differences preserved in time—punctual presence, as Barthes defines the photographic construction of reality—only shows that the condition of the possibility of events and therefore their reproduction is a necessary and inevitable distortion. Each has a "right" interpretation because the "wrong" interpretation occurs with every event, but still without their originals. This should not be some kind of vulgar epistemological relativism. Nietzsche has already clearly demonstrated that history as a history (a reflection of the event as a science of object events) occurs in truth perspectives. There is no multitude of truths. On the contrary, truth rests on the one-time event of a repetition of difference.

From this arises the illusion of the scientific objectivity of history. History in this way may not be the history of the human body as an autonomous history of the world, but only the history of the parent body of the sphere (philosophy, religion, art). As there is no history of media, so there is no history of the body (Flusser 2005). The formation of media bodies in contemporary visual culture denies the autonomy of the media and authorities. In any case, the media always has the tangible presence of the body in its two forms: (1) technical and (2) socio-cultural. We should be able to conclude that the body as a desiring machine, understood in Gilles Deleuze's manner, occurs only with the conceptual performative-media complex formation of life, not as a superior system of governing action, which works by the independent spiritual sphere (philosophy, religion and art). When the body occurs in a performative-conceptual turn of the neo-Avantgarde in the 1960s, we might say that almost every single piece of the world has radically changed the meaning of art, and already it is at work at the end of the history of art (Belting 2002).

6.4   Mediality as a Projection

The event does not happen without a singular-reproductive difference of media. So the body is only then a body when it establishes a living body as the aesthetic emergence of the world. The term means the possibility of the emergence of autonomous and spontaneous events or parts of a whole; however, the complexity of the structure in which there is no determinism or purposeful cause, but the uncertainty of the order of one, became independent in this development, creating a new order. In other words: a case history is not a blind predestination of genotype, but necessarily separate species of the genus in the development of a different phenotype. In this way, it separately changes the structure of the initial substance. The body as a media creation changes the order of cause–effect in the complexity of the emergent order. Whatever happens, the place of the body is established beyond the traditional image of man as a subject-substance of anthropology and humanism. The performative-conceptual turn in contemporary art radically eliminated boundaries between life and art. It might be said that being between life and art is no longer possible in any other way than by establishing the conceptual difference between the body as a living presence and body art events as media-constructed differences. Showing two bodies as the two worlds of life and art takes its place in the singular aestheticization of the world. It stems from the techno-scientific new construction of reality. Therefore, the emergence of a new spirit should be characterized by the bio-technological meaning of a posthuman creature/thing (robot–cyborg–android) which transforms the dual nature of human artifice. The event never occurs without the presence of language–speech–body content: subjects/actors, performances and interactive participants in certain media projections of the world. Subjects/participants are artists of performative practices (visual artists, theatre artists, musicians, dancers, fashion models). Interactive participants are an interim board of viewers, listeners, readers (the audience in the traditional sense of the public artwork), who deal with the world as a projection concept combining performative acts as an event of artistic action and practice. This triad, however, can be a different call. But it is evident that in the contemporary philosophy of art, aesthetics and the theory of contemporary art, there is always a question of who or what has ontological primacy: the artist, the work or the audience?

Heidegger's traditional approach to the formal work of art as a self-installing truth-to-work (*Sich-ins-Werk-setzen der Wahrheit*) opened the question of the end of the subject/object and contemporary art in the coming time. Moreover, the question about the disappearance of complex subject–object relations in the wasteland of the nihilism of contemporary art as art itself was on the blandishments of the world: between the body as work and the body as an event of art has gone to primordial art. The drying process was performed to match the art as did Duchamp's readymade aesthetic object dryers for bottles. When art no longer has its essence or substance of the metaphysical Being and time, something uncanny is turning over the entire assemblage. Heidegger in the 1930s in his analysis of the concept of the event (*Ereignis*) said that doing more does not mean giving the possibility of Being in an epochal-historical sense. As performed in a time which has gone away, the end of the history simultaneously leading to another perspective of thinking. What remains as the aftermath might be the appropriation of the events of being human by nothing that more evidently has a foundation in the reign of beings (Heidegger 2003b: 1–74; Seubold 2005; Young 2001).

The artist as a subject belongs to the creation of works of a modern paradigm in the horizon of the representation of living creatures. Its role lies in the creation of a restoration of the divine world. In the coming contemporary art and the artist, the community that monitors the work itself is no longer an active or passive co-creator. Openness itself acts as a truth being spoken by the artist and his audience about the time and telling the truth about being. We might say that it is a work in its "autonomy", and that it was removed from the author and the audience and vice versa. In its approaching–distancing act it opens from hiding the deepest mysteries of Being and time. A Greek temple and a Christian cathedral belong to the space of art-work at the time of a cult festival. The museum as an idea, quite the contrary, cannot be anything but the triumph of re-historicism. Collecting and preserving works of art from the past because of the awareness of art-historical time realizes its aim by turning the present into a pseudo-event. New visual art in 3D digital images has the ability to visualize the sound of a prehistoric land. In this way, it creates an atmosphere of the technosphere as pseudo-scenery. Each such event in the film industry today occurs in the spectacular empire of emptiness.

Contemporary art, thus, is no longer necessarily an assemblage of many great works that are worthy of some plausible kind of eternity, but many artefacts from the surrounding world of information and communication technologies. Rather than work, there is an inoperative community of the body in interaction with itself. The triad of artists, works and spectators is replaced with the audience in the performative-conceptual turn of the contemporary art event with a triad of language–speech–body. In the openness of the situation and context that are predefined, but also changeable and temporary, the body is always socially and culturally embodied in the language and speech subversion of the society of the control. Art as an event of truth in speech, body language subject/actors in the community, becomes more important than the materiality of images, sculpture, text, recorded music. From Dadaism to Cage's aleatory music leads the way made up of differences in those very same art events—experiment and research, no more blanks or absence of physical presence, but the very nihilistic processing of one uncanny powerful Nothing. Contemporary art is dancing on the edge of nihilism. That is exactly why it can be argued that the performative-conceptual turn in contemporary art from the time of Duchamp's transformations to nowadays, with its own body without work in the event as the first and last "truth" of art and life, keeps within itself something very uncanny and confidential. How and why should we be able to think of that event as ecstatic and immanent, but a non-event from itself, and not outwardly and vertically as a sign of something else and different? Is it not time, paradoxically, for Duchamp's identity transformation in his body to reign the world as the transformation of the appliance multiplied by the non-subjugated freedom of life itself? Does a performative rebellion of the body in contemporary art not ultimately become merely aesthetic staging without any differences between the two simultaneous worlds—technosphere and biosphere?

It is not uncommon, therefore, to talk about contemporary social and cultural practices in a series of "shift" (*turn*) and "reversal" (*Wende*) regarding the performative inversion that occurs in (1) philosophy of language, semiotics, structural linguistics, deconstruction and various versions of pragmatism; (2) sociological disciplines, ethnology and cultural anthropology to social rituals and celebrations to understand the basis of the dramaturgy of community life in performance; (3) dramatology and theatre and visual arts, in which instead of text, speech and body image there only appear speech and imaging projection and the other different ways of interpretation. Generally speaking, we should conclude that it could be overall a result of the dissolution of metaphysical systems of the domination of the *logos* as speech and language over the image of the body itself in the present time. The performative society of contemporary global capitalism thus determines the flexibility and fluidity of network activity rather than a fixed identity. So plurality becomes much more significant than homogeneity. In this way, the concept of performance, although the term itself is like the umbrella that links language–speech–body, uses a variety of scientific disciplines on man and society, applying the pragmatic use of the areas of society and culture, and even includes economics, politics, science and sport. Each performative event in the world takes place as a cultural practice of changes in the body in the space of real-time networking. Therefore, contemporary society has become a non-representational performance spectacle. It represents nothing more, nor any social role, but takes place in the process of staging and theatricalizing the lifestyle experience as the identity of the subject/actor. Since there cannot be a stricter separation of contemporary art from society, politics and culture, as the performative-conceptual turn of contemporary art is just a radical change in the body itself in performance and projections, it is self-evident that the space of theatricalizing and staging of the body refers to the totality of life in general. However, from that point of view, we should make a conceptual distinction between life as a single and unique event in the emergence of the body, and freedom of action and life as a technological play in supervising bodily freedom.

As an analogy, as there are two bodies and two contemporary art worlds (biosphere and technosphere), there are also two lives. The first principle of existence is the biopower body, and the other is the apparatus or biopolitical *dispositif* of society, politics and ideology. Biopolitics acts by freedom of the living body of man obeying other, aesthetic and political purposes of the supervisory or even totalitarian societies of spectacle. Giorgio Agamben thus defines contemporary politics in notions of the performativity theory of new media:

Politics is the exhibition of mediality; it is the act of making a means visible as such. Politics is the sphere neither of an end in itself nor of means subordinated to an end; rather, it is the sphere of a pure mediality without end intended as the field of human action and of human thought. (Agamben 2000: 115–116)

In line with the previous distinction between the two bodies/worlds/ lives of contemporary art, it should be noted that the notion of performance as theatricalizing life within post-dramatic theatre refers to the immediate area of the body itself, the performativity of speech and visual arts in the staging of the living body as a conceptual setup in the context of the extra-institutional and institutional performance of contemporary art. In both the theatre and museum in modern times there are areas of the body exposed to interact with other bodies (participant or spectator performance), and not as a place to present and display body art. What another body, life and the world of contemporary art make of the performative, conceptual mediality of society/government, politics and ideology should be regarded as the event or spectacle of non-representation of the world of global biopolitics. Another body, the world and life are full reifications and a reproductive projection of the power of life itself in the state of surveillance. Paradoxically, allowing the freedom of artistic events runs in basically all possible areas, because under the surveillance of the technosphere as another biosphere or another life is always controlled by global capitalism's "subversive". This is outrageous and uncanny. It is also the reason why contemporary art denotes a visual paradigm of the success of global capitalism. Finally, it reflects spectacular architectural buildings such as museums from Bilbao to Graz and readymade digital economies such as new appliances in information and communication technologies, like the iPod and the smartphone, tablets and gadgets. As a performative act of policy in the mediality of the world of the technosphere, so it was quite expected that at the time of the end of history (of art)—and that means from the original Berlin and Zurich Dadaism to the neo-avant-garde movement of the 1960s and the recent re-enactment and transmediality—performance art will be characterized by the synthesis of mysticism and re-politicizing the event of the transformation of life itself.

What happens in this process of false synthesis of the living body and the reproductive power of the techno-scientific production of aesthetic objects? First of all, the performativity of language, speech and performance as the performativity of the body in contemporary art necessarily becomes a discursive concept of action, culturally different speech and the conceptuality of the body as an open machine/appliance/dispositive acting in the transformation. When we are talking about false synthesis, then it is sure in advance that the two bodies of contemporary art (and the life-world) are the aesthetic objectification of the body in the form of cyborgs, robots and androids, as the ultimate limits of the posthuman body in the digital environment of media consciousness. Language has the power to change the effectiveness of the state of matter only if the body is always already conceptually determined by its uncertainty, or by the emergent properties of spontaneous production of the event. The fundamental feature of the event at this timeline of the ecstasy "moment" merely lies in the coming uncertainty. This is the aporia of the entire pragmatics of language in the performative arts. Language as a condition of possibility of speech in de Saussure's structural linguistics, and in the concept of Derrida's semiological difference (*différance*), is not there more than anywhere else in the world a stable structure of communication between the entities/actors of the singular event (Mersch 2010a). In other words, language and speech may be of significance as de-corporealized in the extreme physical theatre of "blood and tears", to follow Artaud. But it works as a machine-organized order of reality and meaning when it is technically destroyed. In the semiotics of new media, pragmatic meaning should be decisive to interactive communication among participants of an event. In addition, the destruction of language does not mean anything else than that the body in contemporary art appears as an object, machine perception and projection of the world. Duchamp's transformation from the cycle of *Standard Stoppages* credibly demonstrates the limits of this process of destruction of language and objectification of the body as a machine of organized screening.

All the performed techniques of Dadaism such as logic and aleatoric are not just methods or procedures of the destruction of works in radical deconstruction. These are concepts that establish a new order of meaning. So they arise from the assembly language of the body–speech–event in the absolute corporeality of the body. In the performative-conceptual turn, therefore, the body is a machine quite perfectly designed and well organized. In other words, the performance of the body is not only conceptually defined by its gender/sex and other differential features. It might be, rather, a specific situation and context in which only difference exists. To make a difference as the difference was possible, but it is necessary that there is always what makes the difference and products. Therefore, the elimination of "nature" in the performative act, in terms of the identity politics of gender/sex and the subversion of social roles as simultaneously Other, means destroying the "culture". However, the body might not be a cultural formation in the historical situation and the action which changes the context of society, politics and ideology. Rather, we may have a good intention to reach out to the radical form of identity as irreducibly Other differences quite before any possible kind of identity.

Furthermore, a distinction previously provided opportunities of mysticism in the politicization of performativity, because "yes" (*quod*) and "what" (*quid*) created a political-ideological context and situation, for example denoting a systematic racial-discursive violence against immigrants which belongs to different cultures in contemporary Western societies. In whatever terms, the body, other than its overdetermination of the speech and language of the structural power of society, politics and ideology, has an existential-ontological feature of the project of freedom. Finally, it is indefinite in the process of performance. And also, this remains the fundamental difference between the body and its theatricalizing drama and the performativity of the body and its performance. Everything is clear in advance of the metaphysical drama concerning Antigone to the body of Jesus Christ. But nothing makes it possible to predict what happens when it comes to the performativity of the contemporary event in the very body of the biosphere. If this is true, then the freedom of the body in the act of contemporary art as the performative-conceptual turn of the coming event as a real future that Derrida's notion of time has decisive significance at all. Derrida, in fact, marks a difference between the future and the upcoming (*l'avenir*; Derrida 1983). While the former is determined from actuality (the present), can be delivered (due), placed in an order or way that it should happen, the latter denotes the coming of something uncanny or someone who is not really expected. It would not be uncommon to conclude that the future designates the concept of the techno-scientific formation of the body as an aesthetic object (body as readymade), and the upcoming event might be the performative-conceptual turn from the body itself and the projection of the unexpected. This difference is a matter of life and death in contemporary art. If it is gone, then there will be nothing more than the pure aestheticization of life or, quite simply—nothingness in advance.

6.5   Conclusion

What can be inferred from that? First, the relationship between the two bodies of contemporary art at the same time poses the question of relations between the two worlds (language and images) from which Duchamp to the present determines the relationship of life and art as a performative-conceptual turn. The difference between the body as the vagueness and uncertainty of life itself and the body as an aesthetic object ready for use is the difference between freedom and control over freedom. The first place belongs to the living world and the emergence of action during the upcoming suspense. Paradoxically, the performative act grounded in pragmatic events in a moment of "now" and "here" transforms the situation and context as the "fate" of a given society, of guidance, policy and ideology. It does so not by creating anything in advance, unless it is immersed in radically changing the present understanding of actuality. Contemporary art is one that leaves the artist as genius and his audience as fans in favour of artistic works in the open event. Evidently the origin of these settings—of course, Heidegger's thought that was against the "frenzy without consolation" of modern technology—might be the only salvation of the "necessary possibility" of art that comes from the future, as the artwork itself works in an event of opening just another history. Without the openness of historical time, contemporary art is left to the mercy of its own, without meaning and without art (*Kunstlosigkeit*) in the world, which has gone to the anxious abandonment of man and earth, gods and mortals. Therefore, performative art can be the last call for the "truth" of life as art in the body without structural additions, in the body without the aesthetic illusion of pseudo-transformation, in the body without the spectacle of the world as the medial reproduction event. Instead of transcendent "meaning" the language of metaphysics, performative art is not explained by reference to another meaning (symbolic or connotative).

It is simply "there" as a world without the language of metaphysics is just "here", immanent, though bare and no longer supporting the divine in terms of theology and religion. It simply "does" in its primal vagueness, like that "white eschatology" that Benjamin finds in the inability of Baroque allegory to reach a state of fullness of emptiness. Moreover, it neutralizes any possible gaps in the identification and definition of its secret past. Performance art does not work anymore, as it is customary to think in an abstract instantaneous time without it supporting either the past or the future. Quite the contrary, it is a living rebellion versus the actuality of the self-installation-in-picture of the aesthetic object, which always has the face of media nullity, as is well known from pop art and Andy Warhol. The media projection of the body at the scene of an event in the performative-conceptual turn can only think of the transformation of predefined limits, terms, definitions of reproduction, replication and cloning. For the coming or not coming, any more uncanny than the rule of the machine to produce the world as an aesthetic object in the form of the cognitive memory of an event, or a coming event that no one can predict, or think otherwise than as a mythopoetic dream of freedom of the disembodied presence of the cosmic spheres, which vibrate in their circularity and flicker like light passing through the crystals. *Tertium non datur.*

The event of contemporary art is an act of Duchamp played a radical transformation in his two fatal body-world-life. What else needs to be in the transition period in a post-Duchamp era? The prerequisite for entry into a truly new era is perhaps too difficult for "our" time without words. To be able to think and live the true art of the coming era needs to totally destroy the aesthetics of each and every event in which ethics rests on the illusion of freedom and the separation of body and reproduction apparatus as a machine. Without it, we will, otherwise, witness the constantly "new" killing of the dead shadow of Duchamp and his transformation in the guise of "new" language and body image. It may be aesthetically pleasing, even if apparently shocking and morbid, as the performance of transgression, cannibalism and humanism, pornography and eroticism, obscenity and abjection. Performative art in all its forms is an event of contemporary art from life and its transition to a contemporary aesthetic drive where all those monsters exist and, otherwise, we serve as such—the capitalist machine of consumption and enjoyment of the body. Behind its mask, there is nothing more sublime or mysterious.

In a film directed by Andrei Tarkovsky, *Stalker*, all that remains alive in the event of apocalyptic and totalitarian threats to humankind in the function and structure of bare life (stuff) should be nothing other than listening to the rain-soaked earth's vibrations and mud. Breathing the land and listening to the voice fit beyond this world that is not "ours", not "anybody's", because it no longer constitutes a language rather than its technical devices and tools, because such a world no longer exists in any other way than in a performative-conceptual turn of a released uncanny body condemned to roam its own wastes and the pit looking for meaning. Without language, art no longer makes sense and does not need more than a pure consolation, because that was the other side of the historical development of the myth through religion to science. In fact, apart from the sensible view of the absolute idea (God?) would be the consolation of the terrible power to conquer life, survival and emergency chains of the boredom of existence. When art is the only thing left to be a consolation as such, it is apparent that there was a total time of the reign of aestheticizing the world as the pleasure of spending all that remains. Bataille's sovereign economy challenged this kind of victim. Performative art, thus, arises in its most radical achievements of the sacrifice of the body against any possible mystical re-politicization of art. Whoever enters his holy flesh into the secular order of society, politics and ideology and its uncomfortable protection of the institutional order of modern art (museums, galleries, theatres) not only risks his life symbolically, but first the order of life as art, which rests on the institutionalization of "normality", "morality," "nature and culture". Freedom in our unconditional lack of foundation is nothing other than the event in the abyss of freedom itself and requires immediate action in the only single body. This death is represented as the immanent limits of performative art. It may be uncanny, just as a conceptual field, the abolition of the world as an aesthetic object, only happens as the embodiment of the things in human life. Or, more simply, when things breathe in our life, someone else breathes a soul, which is the image/object of a conceptual performance by Anselm Kiefer from the *Stelle Cadente* cycles, where gloves of the yellow colour of gold under glass as subversive traces invoke the history of a different world beyond sinister ideology and death. Performative art denotes, therefore, a challenge to the contemporary age, because there is no valuable comprehension of the sacrifice of life and holiness. However, it encompasses the ideological-political use of victims for every possible secular purpose—from terrorism, torture and biopolitical production to all aesthetic objects. For this challenge as an event, the coming mysteries are yet to be appropriately prepared intellectually and experientially. There is no royal road to the last secrets of art that exceed their limits of authority as an epochal work in the event of performance practice. Every single time might be only making a journey of freedom without any pre-known object and any kind of aim and purpose.

Note

1. "Dadaism is a movement of 'mystical', not political actions, despite the public statements of political and sharpness of its actions" (Mersch 2010b).

References

Adorno, Theodor W. 1973. *Negative Dialektik*. Frankfurt/M: Suhrkamp.

Agamben, Giorgio. 1999. *The Man Without Content*. Translated from Italian by Georgia Albert. Stanford, CA: Stanford University Press.

———. 2000. *The Means Without End: Notes on Politics*. Translated from Italian by Vincenzo Binetti and Cesare Casarino. Minneapolis and London: University of Minnesota Press.

———. 2009. *What is an Apparatus? And Other Essays*. Translated from Italian by David Kishik and Stefan Pedatella. Stanford, CA: Stanford University Press.

Alberro, Alexander. 2003. *Conceptual Art and the Politics of Publicity*. Cambridge, MA and London: The MIT Press.

Baudrillard, Jean. 1998. *The Consumer Society. Myths and Structures*. London: SAGE Publications.

Beller, Jonathan. 2006. *The Cinematic Mode of Production: Attention Economy and the Society of the Spectacle*. Dartmouth College Press.

Belting, Hans. 2002. *Das Ende der Kunstgeschichte? Eine Revision nach Zehn Jahren.* 2nd ed. Munich: C.H. Beck.

Beroš, Nada. 2006. *Dalibor Martinis: Public Secrets.* Zagreb: Museum of Contemporary Art/Omnimedia.

Deleuze, Gilles. 1964. *Proust et le signes.* Paris: Ed. Minuit.

Derrida, Jacques. 1983. *Dissemination.* Translated from French by Barbara Johnson. Chicago: University of Chicago Press.

Fischer-Lichte, Erika. 2004. *Ästhetik des Performativen.* Frankfurt/M: Suhrkamp.

Flusser, Vilém. 2005. *Medienkultur.* Frankfurt/M: S. Fischer.

Foucault, Michel. 1980. *Power/Knowledge. Selected Interviews and Other Writings 1972–1977,* ed. C. Gordon. New York: Pantheon Books.

Groys, Boris. 2003. *Topologie der Kunst.* Munich: C. Hanser.

———. 2010. Marx after Duchamp, or the Artist's Two Bodies. *e-flux Journal,* No. 19, October.

Guattari, Felix. 2009. To Have Done with a Massacre of the Body. In *Chaosophy: Texts and Interviews 1972–1977,* 207–214. Los Angeles, CA: Semiotext(e).

Heidegger, Martin. 2003a. Die Zeit des Weltbildes. In *Holzwege.* Frankfurt/M: V. Klostermann.

———. 2003b. Der Ursprung des Kunstwerkes. In *Holzwege.* Frankfurt/M: V. Klostermann.

Kittler, Friedrich A. 2002. *Optische Medien.* Berlin: Merve.

Lacoue-Labarthe, Philippe. 1998. *Typography. Mimesis, Philosophy, Politics.* Stanford, CA: Stanford University Press.

Lyotard, Jean-François. 1988. *The Differend: Phrases in Dispute.* Translated from French by Georges van dem Abbeele. Manchester: Manchester University Press.

———. 1990. *Duchamp's TRANS/formers.* Translated from French by Ian McLeod. Venice, CA: The Lapise Press.

Massumi, Brian. 2002. The Evolutionary Alchemy of Reason: Stelarc. In *Parables for the Virtual. Movement, Affect, Sensation.* Durham, NC and London: Duke University Press.

———. 2011. *Semblance and Event. Activist Philosophy and Occurrent Arts.* Cambridge, MA and London: The MIT Press.

Mersch, Dieter. 2002. *Ereignis und Aura. Untersuchungen zu einer Ästhetik des Performativen.* Frankfurt/M: Edition Suhrkamp.

———. 2010a. *Posthermeneutik.* Deutsche Zeitschrift für Philosophie, Sonderbande, Vol. 26. Berlin: Akademie Verlag.

———. 2010b. Kunst und Sprache. Hermeneutik, Dekonstruktion, und die Ästhetik des Ereignens. [Online] Accessed November 20, 2018. http://www.scribd.com/document/39404340/Mersch-kunst-und-Sprache.

Paić, Žarko. 2005. *A Politics of Identity: The Culture as a New Ideology.* Zagreb: Editions Antibarbarus.

—————. 2006. *A Picture without the World: The Iconoclasm of Contemporary Art.* Zagreb: Litteris.

—————. 2011. *Posthuman Condition: The End of Man and Odds of Other History.* Zagreb: Litteris.

Puchner, Martin. 2006. *Poetry of the Revolution. Marx, Manifestos, and the Avant-Gardes.* Princeton, NJ: Princeton University Press.

Seubold, Günther. 2005. *Kunst als Enteignis. Heidegger's Weg zu einer nicht mehr metaphysischen Denken.* Bonn: DenkMal Verlag.

Virilio, Paul. 1991. *The Aesthetics of Disappearance.* Cambridge, MA and London: The MIT Press.

Young, Julian. 2001. *Heidegger's Philosophy of Art.* Cambridge: Cambridge University Press.

Žižek, Slavoj, ed. 1994. *Mapping Ideology.* London and New York: Verso.

7

Conclusion

The answer to the question of the essence of the image in the era of the technosphere is foreseen in advance. The image does not have its essence anymore, as there is no clear difference between object and observer. Exactly because of that, we must start addressing intensity instead of essence and, instead of the symbolic power of painting, we should bring in the possibilities of the meaning of the image in the process of incurring a new work/event beyond reason and comprehension. We no longer grasp the image from its emanation that emerged from the divinity of a sacred source. Now at our disposal should be an array of cognitive tools with which we seek to determine how an image is generated and how its power of fascination occurs in the situation and context without initial cause and ultimate purpose: from visual semiotics to image science, from digital aesthetics to cybernetics and post-phenomenology. Already with quantum theory, the uncertainty principles in Werner Heisenberg's physics, and especially after the introduction of Claude Shannon's mathematical theory of communication as the beginning of the absolute cybernetization of life and the transition to a technical construction of reality, it has become evident that a complex relationship of overlapping and mutual conditionality occurs between the observer and the observed

Ž. Paić, *White Holes and the Visualization of the Body*,
https://doi.org/10.1007/978-3-030-14467-8_7

object. The disappearance of the subject in contemporary philosophy and art assuredly begins with this significant cognitive and theoretical revelation of "nature as becoming". Specifically, the latter does not "really" exist without an object as the relationship/bond of thought and motion. It is obvious that the image thereby has lost all of the metaphysical properties that were attributed to it throughout art history: from imitation and presentation (*mimesis*) to representation (*representatio*).

This book is primarily intended to lead to a paradigm shift after the end of metaphysics in cybernetics, as Heidegger first made transparent in his late thinking. When the concept of the plan of immanence came to the place of transcendence, or when Deleuze and Guattari by the notion of the desiring machine reversed the entire legacy of Freud's and Lacan's psychoanalysis, then the *corporeal turn* reached the stage of realization in the technological construction of the world at large. The image precedes language as digital simulation precedes the phenomenon of a new cognitive reflection of things in the technical environment of artificial life. Through the six previous chapters I have attempted to expose my understanding of the visualization of the body as a path which necessarily goes beyond the theoretical orientations that the body has thought of "from above" or "from below" (theology, phenomenology and psychoanalysis). Without a philosophical insight into how the technosphere presupposes the elimination of binary oppositions like nature versus culture, mind/soul versus body and so on, it might be impossible to reach a different way of thinking such that we cannot think of the body any longer like "the obscure object of desire", as it suggests the title of an intriguing movie directed by Luis Buñuel. Briefly, what becomes a matrix of new thinking is not a biologically established body in the extensions of mechanical technology, but the body in the posthuman framework of cross-linked interactions, the body without organs that arises from the logic of the action performed by digital constructivism. By visualizing the body, we reach out into the space of singularity of thought that is not a mere description of reality, but its aesthetic construction, designing the world by models of its own desires for immaterial forms and shapes of crystals.

In the introductory chapter, I already pointed out that this denaturalization process of life has radical consequences for understanding body and technology relationships. When sexuality is superseded by pornography, desire becomes lust or a mere fulfilment of needs that are multiplied and networked in the same way as bodies in communication with other bodies. This interconnectivity in the network of events takes on the features of the mere transfer of desire to dematerialize the object. Thus, the royal power of the subject, which modern metaphysics inherited from Kant to Hegel, goes to the state of emptiness and disappearance of the reason for the "revolution" of that assemblage which Lyotard called, in the traces of Freud, the libidinal economy. There is no doubt that phenomenology and psychoanalysis in the work of Merleau-Ponty and Lacan deserve to put the body at the centre of reflection of the world after the end of its metaphysical possibilities. But neither the body as the open object of the view nor the mere image-transforming desire nor the unconscious articulated as language can any longer be the key to understanding the technosphere. Simply, it is not a problem in the world as consciousness, but in digital simulation and the construction of virtual worlds. Hence, there is a cut that separates Being from the event with which artificial life is born as a biopolitical production in the form of a desiring machine. It is therefore not surprising that in contemporary art we are witnessing the reign of the process, the project and the experiment, the aesthetics of the event, and no longer a fixed artistic work. An exhaustive analysis has shown that Lacan and Deleuze, in particular, liberated the space for a different view of the subject. Nothing has any longer the power to establish the order of things beyond the matrix of what appears when the magma of life goes beyond the metaphysical machine of history. Indeed, if to be meant to think and to say the same, the event means a change of state, it is the inability to stop a machine that visualizes life itself as a performative-conceptual trace of time without the primordial meaning of history.

Finally, if language no longer speaks of a world because it has nothing more to say, but it leaves the visualization of events, it is obvious that this world of interconnected bodies without organs should be understood from a quite other and different perspective. In the last chapter, therefore, I tried to see how within the space and the time of contemporary art the possibility of thinking of the body from its unwavering freedom of self-exposure and self-reflection developed. In addition to the dominant approaches to this problem from the horizons of post-phenomenology and the re-enactment of the process of re-confrontation with the trauma of the Real as the bond of Lacan's psychoanalysis and the re-politicization of art, it seems to me that the facts should be reversed. Instead of body corporeality, it might be necessary to go one step further and acknowledge that the singularity of an object requires overcoming the world as the empire of objects and living space without being controlled from the outside or from the inside. What does that really mean? When it is all repeating itself at an increasing intensity of power, then at the scene occurs the power of difference in the form of an event which, as compared to the previous history of metaphysics, does not reside in the *logos*. The mad search for the meaning of life in the time of technically produced reality requires a kind of creative chaos as a system with which we subvert the order built on the paradoxical desire for capital as the backbone of history. Nothing can stand up to this world of constructive amazement except the desire for freedom as an event without any dependence on the foundation and reason for existence. If your body is your creative construct of singularity, then its visualization might be just a sign of the last secret of the spectacle.

Seeing does not mean having a Being. Owning a picture of its own thinking means being photographed at the time of the disappearance of the visible world, when information such as the astral body disappears in "white holes" on the empty horizon of the infinite sky. It seems that only what is left might be in the close encounter with the mystery of what we call the digital world and its deceptive shadows.

Index[1]

---

[1] Note: Page numbers followed by 'n' refer to notes.

© The Author(s) 2019
Ž. Paić, *White Holes and the Visualization of the Body*,
https://doi.org/10.1007/978-3-030-14467-8

CPSIA information can be obtained
at www.ICGtesting.com
Printed in the USA
LVHW031833090519
617270LV00010B/284/P